BY ERWIN RAPHAEL McMANUS

The Genius of Jesus
The Way of the Warrior
The Last Arrow
Wide Awake
Soul Cravings
Stand Against the Wind
The Artisan Soul
The Barbarian Way
Uprising
Chasing Daylight
An Unstoppable Force

THE GENIUS
OF JESUS

THE GENIUS
OF JESUS

*The Man Who
Changed Everything*

ERWIN RAPHAEL
McMANUS

CONVERGENT

NEW YORK

Published in the United States by Convergent Books, an imprint of
Random House, a division of Penguin Random House LLC, New York.

CONVERGENT BOOKS is a registered trademark and its C colophon
is a trademark of Penguin Random House LLC.

LIBRARY OF CONGRESS CATALOGING-IN-PUBLICATION DATA
Names: McManus, Erwin Raphael, author.
Title: The genius of Jesus / Erwin Raphael McManus.
Description: New York: Convergent, [2021]
Identifiers: LCCN 2021012922 (print) | LCCN 2021012923 (ebook) |
ISBN 9780593137383 (hardcover) | ISBN 9780593137390 (ebook)
Subjects: LCSH: Jesus Christ—Example. | Genius.
Classification: LCC BT304.2 .M36 2021 (print) | LCC BT304.2 (ebook) |
DDC 232—dc23
LC record available at lccn.loc.gov/2021012922
LC ebook record available at lccn.loc.gov/2021012923

Printed in Canada on acid-free paper

crownpublishing.com

2 4 6 8 9 7 5 3 1

First Edition

Book design by Victoria Wong

As I write these words we have not yet formally
been introduced.

We will meet soon but the love affair has already
begun.

You are the daughter of my daughter and that
means that you are doubly loved.

You spent your first year growing inside of the
most extraordinary human you will ever know.

The scriptures tell us that before you were born,
God knew you. Before you took your first breath,
he called you out.

He gave you to the best dad and mom you could
ever hope for. We call them Jake and Mariah.

He gave you an uncle named Aaron McManus,
who will always be there for you.

He gave you an aunt named Paty, and her family
can't wait to meet you.

He gave you to an incredible family from whom
you get the name Goss.

They are from Arkansas and they love you as
much as we do.

And of course he gave you your grandma Kim,
who adores you already. She will be your favorite.

Me . . . I'm your grandpa. My name is Erwin.

I wrote this book for you.

Before you take your first breath I want you to know you're a genius.

There has never been, nor will there ever be, born on this earth, anyone like you.

You are unique. One of a kind.

Welcome to the world. We need you here.

Never question how much you are loved.

Just like the oxygen you will breathe with every breath (never thinking about it twice) so will you forever be surrounded by and enveloped by love.

Our love and the unfailing love Jesus has for you will always be there for you.

Never forget that God is love and that you have been created as an object of his love.

He is the source of all your soul will ever long for in this life.

I hope you read this book one day and that it helps you discover your own genius.

But if you forget everything I have written in this book,

please never forget this . . .

I love you.

Salvi

Contents

THE GENIUS
OF JESUS

CHAPTER ONE

The Genius

I have spent my entire adult life studying genius and searching for God. I always saw those pursuits as mutually exclusive: one a question of human potential, and the other a matter of faith. But the longer you live, the more you begin to realize that things you once thought were disparate narratives in your life were actually always interwoven. My fascination with genius and my openness to God were both rooted in a desperate search for something to translate my life from the mundane to the transcendent.

Although my search was academic, it was always far more personal. Growing up, I felt trapped within my own limitations, and I longed to find a path to a higher, better self. I was Peter Parker before the radioactive spider bit him. I hoped there was something extraordinary within me, within all of us, that could transform us to our most heroic selves.

Most of my friends envied athletes, or musicians, or actors. I envied philosophers, scientists, and inventors—anyone who could see something that was invisible to everyone else. I could live with someone being faster, or stronger, or smarter than me. I just didn't want to be blind to the endless possibilities of the unknown.

The fear, of course, was that there was no genius within me to be found—no God who could awaken my originality, or at least make up for my lack of it. One thing I have learned over my lifetime: We search for what we lack, and we long for what we fear we don't possess. I longed to be more than a meaningless composite of carbon. So I became a student of genius and an explorer in search of God.

I am convinced that when we experience expressions of genius, it elevates our own personal capacity. Once you see it done, you know it's possible. When one human accomplishes the extraordinary, it becomes a measure for all who follow them. Would Kobe Bryant have become a superstar if there had been no Michael Jordan? Would there be a Stephen Hawking if there had not been an Albert Einstein? Would there be an Elon Musk if there had not been a Nikola Tesla? Greatness inspires greatness. Genius provokes genius.

There are a handful of people who consistently make

the list of history's greatest geniuses. My list always begins with Leonardo da Vinci, the quintessential Renaissance man. His genius touched nearly every field of human endeavor. He was an inventor, artist, architect, scientist, musician, mathematician, sculptor, engineer, astronomer, botanist, cartographer, and so much more. He was a futurist of unparalleled insight, foreshadowing the invention of the submarine and the helicopter. Although he only completed fifteen works of art throughout his lifetime, he is considered perhaps the greatest painter of all time.

There are so many others who come to mind. In the arena of music, Wolfgang Amadeus Mozart and Ludwig van Beethoven used the same twelve notes to generate the complexity, beauty, and artistry of classical music. In the field of science, there are Albert Einstein, Marie Curie, and more recently Stephen Hawking. In film, the directors Orson Welles and Alfred Hitchcock set the bar for transcendent storytelling. In the game of chess, there was Bobby Fischer, who set a standard of genius in a game of intellect. In the world of technology and business, we have the undeniable genius of Steve Jobs and Bill Gates.

Each of these individuals has unique attributes that set them apart not only from the rest of the world, but from the best in the world. They saw the world differently. They created a future that would not have existed without them. Like Copernicus and Galileo, they violated our view of reality and forced us to see the world anew. Their ideas have resulted in space travel and solar energy. They have given us a way to fight cancer and a way to save our planet. They have given us the internet and the tools to explore and express our own creativity. Once we saw the world through their eyes, we could never see the world the same way again.

The concept of genius was birthed in the writings of the Greek philosophers. In Plato's works, Socrates speaks of the daemons that inspire the genius of great men. From medicine to mathematics, from philosophy to physics, the Greeks were a fountainhead of accomplishment. Their world was the birthplace of Homer, Pythagoras, Euclid, Hippocrates, Aristotle, Archimedes, and, of course, Alexander the Great. For them, genius was awakened when the divine touched the human—those moments when the heroes of old rose above the status of ordinary men. Some expressions of human creativity were so transcendent, they could only be attributed to the gods.

By the time of the Roman Empire, the cast of genius had become more concrete. The Romans attributed genius to a place or a person's position, rather than to the person themselves. It was assumed that simply being crowned Caesar meant a person carried the mark of genius, an assumption that history has proved flatly wrong. Still, the Romans were perceptive in noticing that a person was neither a genius nor the possessor of genius. We are possessed by genius. It's something given to us—something entrusted to us. Genius was seen as an endowment that came or went at the whim of the gods.

Genius is inseparable from the creative process. The word "genius" is expressive of the capacity to be generative. The genius gives birth to something new. The genius creates. The mark of true genius is that the impossible becomes possible. The unknowable becomes knowable. The invisible becomes visible. The genius speaks the future into existence. Genius expresses itself in every domain in which humans create. Wherever there is a field of human accomplishment, there is potential for the expression of genius.

The genius does not always have the highest IQ, the best education, or even the most comprehensive knowledge of their field. But their combination of originality, imagination, creativity, perspective, passion, and intelligence merge together to help them see the world differently—and then create a different world. While we often attribute the title of "genius" to an individual, that designation only comes as a result of the extraordinary nature of their work. There must be something we can point to and describe as a genuine work of genius. Yet these works of genius are rarely acknowledged by their contemporaries. Often geniuses are met with jealousy and resistance from their peers. This is in no small part due to the fact that genius is often accompanied by self-indulgence, irrational compulsion, and perhaps even a touch of madness. And if all genius is touched by madness, then it is also touched by the divine.

As I studied genius in college, hoping to unlock my own fleeting sense of purpose, I ran into Jesus of Nazareth. Unexpectedly, my pursuit of genius and my search for God converged in one person: the most transformative human being who ever lived.

I AM ALWAYS perplexed when I consider how my life has been completely changed by one person who lived over two thousand years ago.

The irony, of course, is that I had no idea I was on a journey of faith.

I grew up essentially irreligious, though I always considered myself a deeply spiritual person. It's not that I was untouched by religion; I simply wasn't defined by it.

As immigrants from El Salvador, my family would have considered ourselves Roman Catholic, though our faith was more something we inherited than something we adhered to, in that we rarely attended Mass. For some reason it was important to my mother that all of us be confirmed in the Catholic Church. Around the age of ten, my brother and I went through catechism and confirmation and received our first communion. It was my first experience with organized religion, far from my last.

I was twelve years old when my mother, who has always been intellectually curious, brought home a jade-green Buddha statue. She placed him in a prominent spot in our living room where we would see him as we went about our daily lives. We rubbed his belly for good luck. We really needed some good luck. Looking back now, I realize how difficult my mom's life must have been at the time. In her early twenties, she was already the mother of two boys. Her marriage to my father had ended, and the weight of our futures had fallen completely on her shoulders. She worked as a stewardess for Pan Am to support us and did everything necessary to give us a new life. She must have wondered many times where God was in the midst of all her struggles.

My mother never would have called herself a Buddhist, but she said she bought the statue because she was open to anything that might bring us better luck. Even then it seemed inescapable that our search for faith was deeply connected to our personal struggles in life. My best recollection is that the smiling Buddha didn't last very long. Life got harder. So did faith. One day, in what I imagine was a moment of profound disappointment and frustration, my mom took the Buddha and destroyed it. That was the end of our brief exploration of Eastern mysticism.

A couple of years later, there was a horrific earthquake in Managua, Nicaragua, that killed thousands of people. I remember how shaken my mom was, hearing the news of that natural disaster so close to her home. She expressed to me that she no longer believed in a personal God who was actively involved in human affairs. How could a loving God allow such senseless tragedy? She still believed in God's existence, but she concluded that he was either incapable of helping us or indifferent to our pain and suffering.

She began listening to the teachings of Rabbi Harold Kushner, whose work later emerged in the book *When Bad Things Happen to Good People*. Kushner's philosophy convinced my mother that she was closer to Judaism than to any other religion or belief system. I quickly borrowed her copy of the book and devoured Kushner's writings. I still remember how he explained God's relationship to human suffering. While God was genuinely caring, Kushner taught, he was unfortunately powerless to help us in our times of need. This pretty much matched my experience. If God was out there, he wasn't very helpful.

It seems strange to say, but there was solace in believing God had good intentions toward us, even if they were poorly executed. My mom was drawn to Kushner's progressive expression of Judaism because it explained God's absence in her pain while allowing her to still believe in his goodness. It felt good to know that God was not indifferent to us, just overwhelmed. Still, if this life is more than

God can handle, you have to begin to wonder how in the world we are supposed to survive it.

Looking back, our journey of faith felt much like a man wandering across a desert, moving from water hole to water hole. When we found a new teacher or worldview, our thirst was quenched for a moment, but very quickly we found ourselves parched and desperate again.

My mom's spiritual journey during my most formative years made a huge impact on me. She was earnest in her search for God and for truth. She was always open and curious and optimistic. She was willing to change her mind when she discovered she was mistaken. To this day, she is one of those rare people capable of radical change, even fearless. She was never satisfied with ignorance. If it could be known, she would find a way to discover it.

How we are loved as children influences our capacity to believe in God in our adulthood. If we are raised to be open-minded, curious, and inquisitive, we will have less fear and be less resistant to mystery, uncertainty, and the transcendent. But when our experiences as children convince us that people cannot be trusted, we should not be surprised to find ourselves resistant to ever trusting a God we cannot see and do not know. If we find ourselves the victims of deep pain, disappointment, and disillusionment when we are young, these, too, become significant contributors to our spiritual development. This would definitely describe my childhood. For the sake of others whom I love, I will not go into details here. It is enough to say that many of us walk with a limp from wounds we received when we could barely stand on our own.

This is where I found myself very early on in my own spiritual journey. I wasn't even twelve years old when my mom and stepfather sent me to see a psychiatrist for the first time. I had a sleep disorder—nightmares, sleepwalking, insomnia. I was also failing in school, despondent, and reclusive. My parents saw the symptoms, but it was much worse than they could understand. I was quiet and introverted, the kind of child who spends most of his time hiding in his inner world. Through no fault of anyone else's, I felt deeply disconnected from the people around me, and I struggled with a deep sense of insignificance, which led me down a path of depression and hopelessness. Children have to process adult realities—divorce, abandonment, rejection, failure, abuse—through their limited knowledge and life experience. I lacked the tools to face the harsh realities of the world, and my internal world suffered.

At school I was an outsider, always wondering how everyone but me seemed to have the competencies to belong. I felt this way even with my own family. Either I didn't fit the world, or the world didn't fit me. So I created my own world, a universe in my head. I pictured a new me, a new life, a new world within my imagination. I had so many friends there. I always belonged. I never wanted to leave. That world became so imprinted in my imagination that it stays with me even still.

In time, my way of escaping a life I didn't feel adequate for would become the material for creating a better life and a better world. I pictured the ideals I felt were missing in real life—until one day I found the courage to begin to materialize them. Imagination had been my means of escape. Now it was my means to create.

At the time, though, all I knew was that somewhere, somehow, my soul needed to find healing. Without a language to define it then, I now understand that this was my search for God. I didn't know where to look, so I looked everywhere.

In college I was introduced to Socrates. I was compelled by his search for truth and his love of questions. I also thought it mattered that he was willing to die, and in fact gave his life, for the pursuit of truth. Socrates prepared me for Jesus, who also loved questions and was equally compelled to seek truth at any cost. Yet Jesus went a step further, in that the sacrifice of his life came at a greater cost and was for a greater purpose.

When I consciously began a search for God, for truth, for faith, as an adult, I reflected on my childhood roots in Roman Catholicism. I had attended just enough Mass to have the image of the Crucifixion mark my consciousness. Mass had been held in Latin. Every time you entered the cathedral, it felt as if you stepped back a thousand years in time. The priests wore dramatic robes with brilliant colors and high hats that pointed to the ceiling. Everyone was quiet, and a feeling of reverence filled every inch of the space.

Even as a child, I was fascinated by the symbolism and the rituals that had remained the same over the centuries—though I must admit that the worship always seemed more like a funeral than a wedding. There was communion and confession, but never celebration. Even Jesus seemed to be trapped in misery. The image of the Christ was always one of suffering and sorrow, a man bleeding on a crucifix. I'm sure during Mass someone mentioned that Jesus rose from the dead, but the resurrection was overshadowed by the man hanging on the cross right in front of me. For us, the story of Jesus always ended at the cross. This was Jesus's singular contribution to the world. His was the example of the virtue of suffering.

I never understood how the death of someone who lived so long ago could in any way have significance for my life. Yet there was something profound and beautiful and even romantic around this image that haunted me. It inspired me to consider unimaginable possibilities. If God could become human then anything was possible. More than that, it opened my mind to consider the existence of the transcendent. It compelled me to search for answers I wasn't sure even existed.

Is it possible that there is a God?

Is it possible to know his story?

Is it possible to find God in our own story?

I definitely had a bias. My search was not objective. It was human. I hoped there was more to this life than I had come to know.

If I could find God, maybe I could find the healing my soul longed for as well. If I found God, maybe I could also find the meaning of life. If I found God, maybe I could also find my own path to genius.

I WILL NEVER forget Robert Heinlein's classic book *Glory Road*. This book personified everything I was longing for in my own life. There was a character named Evelyn Cyril Gordon, otherwise known as "Easy" or "Flash." Gordon has no idea what to do with his life when, suddenly, he sees a newspaper ad asking the question, "Are you a coward or are you the hero that we're looking for?"

He responds to the ad and soon is invited on a great quest by an exotic woman named Star. The quest is fraught with danger and dragons, and the probability of Gordon's return is unlikely. His adventures force him to question everything he ever believed to be true, and to open his imagination to things he once thought impossible. Even at the end of the book, when all things have been accomplished, he wonders if it ever really happened. Only in the final pages, when he's invited to take another trip down the Glory Road, does he realize the whole thing was real.

Even in my adolescence I was searching for my "glory road." I hoped that one day someone would call me to an adventure with some kind of cosmic purpose. I wanted my life to matter somehow. I had to believe that there was a hero side of me as well. I wasn't searching for God in hopes of an afterlife. I was searching for God in hopes that there was more to *this* life than simply existing. Looking back now, I can see why, from primary school on, I began studying the works of geniuses.

There seem to be a few consistent characteristics where genius emerges. Genius sees what no one has seen and hears what no one has heard. It explains what could not be understood, creates what could not be imagined. Whatever the genius does with their talents, they do it better than it has ever been done—and, more often than not, make it look easy while doing it.

If I were to make a short list of what marks a genius, I would say:

1. They are heretical.
2. They are original.

3. They are transformative in their field.

4. They are extremist.

They are heretical in that they violate the status quo and challenge our most deeply held beliefs and values. They are original in that they see the world from a perspective that has never existed before. They are transformative in that their lives become a marker of before and after. They are extremists in that they are consumed in their pursuit of the creative act and convinced of the singular importance of their passion.

It seems serendipitous that the concept of genius was being invented around the same time Jesus of Nazareth walked this earth. If the Greeks and Romans were correct in viewing genius as the expression of the divine consuming the human, then Jesus would be the greatest expression of that phenomenon humanity has ever witnessed: a human living in the fullness of the divine. A human being who is both fully present and fully transcendent. Einstein saw a new way to do math. Fischer saw a new way to play chess. Jesus saw a new way to be human, a way to live each moment fully present and fully alive. Imagine if your every choice and every action only and always created the good and the beautiful and the true. The genius of Jesus is that he teaches us how to become human again.

And yet I have never seen a list of history's great geniuses that has included the person of Jesus. How is it possible that Jesus of Nazareth, who singularly changed the course of modern history, would not merit being mentioned among the great minds of the human story? How has the genius of Jesus been so strangely overlooked?

I imagine that this is likely because we feel we must either embrace Jesus as divine or discount him completely. Yet the opposite should be most true. If you do not accept him as divine, then it would seem impossible to deny his genius. How else can you explain that one singular person has so dramatically impacted humanity? Of course, if Jesus is who he claimed to be—if Jesus is God—then his impact on human history would be completely expected.

My decision over forty years ago to surrender myself to the person of Jesus has forever changed the direction of my life. Jesus has singularly impacted my values, my mindset, and the choices I have made. The outcome of that change has made me a better husband, a better father, and without question a better person. Though I am deeply flawed, I cannot deny the tangible changes in my life as a result of my relationship with Jesus.

Simply put, Jesus has made me a better human. Or maybe, Jesus made me human again.

The data goes far beyond my own personal experience. For more than two thousand years, millions of people across the world have been transformed through their faith in Jesus Christ. If you were a cultural anthropologist looking to examine this phenomenon from a purely scientific perspective, you would have a massive sample size. The control group stretches across all of modern history, every economic and educational stratum, and virtually every culture across the face of the earth.

Academics even have a term for how a culture is transformed through belief in Jesus Christ: "redemption and lift." In his book *Underdevelopment Is a State of Mind*, economist Lawrence E. Harrison observed how the Christian mindset had a measurable effect on the economic development and prosperity of societies. His analysis focused not on the ceiling of wealth but the living conditions and well-being of the common citizen. Simply put, certain mindsets and belief systems create the internal psychological mechanisms needed to rise above poverty when the opportunity is given. The valuing of education, the treatment of women, the emergence of an entrepreneurial mindset, personal responsibility for choices: All these were elevated in Christian societies. Harrison was not in any way advocating for the validity of believing in Jesus. He simply identified an economic reality. Even if Jesus is only an idea, that idea changes the way humans approach life. Is there any other idea that has ever brought that kind of change?

From a purely historical perspective, this would have to be identified as a work of genius. But it's a different kind of genius than the one we're primed to spot. Jesus's genius is missed because it is comprehensive rather than contained in a particular discipline.

Genius, as a rule, is not transferable. You could spend your life with Mozart and never become a great composer. You could spend your life with Picasso and never become a great painter. If you spent your life with Michael Jordan, you still wouldn't make it to the NBA unless you were six feet six with a forty-inch vertical.

With Jesus, his genius is dramatically the reverse. His genius, it would seem, is contagious. When you align your heart with Jesus, it begins a process of transformation. Soon you begin to live your life as Jesus would. There is, if I could use the phrase, a transference of genius. Because of Jesus, I have watched people who have been reckless in their relationships begin to value others above themselves. I have seen men overcome a lifetime of arrogance and choose to define their lives by the strength of humility. I have known individuals of significant wealth move from a life of greed to a life of generosity. I have experienced the beautiful transformation of those trapped in depression and hopelessness finding new eyes to see the beauty and wonder of life.

What other ideas have ever demonstrated this kind of transformative power?

Let me be transparent. I fully believe in the divinity of

Jesus and in the historical accuracy of all the scriptures. I believe God stepped into human history, took on flesh and blood, and walked among us, and that his name is Jesus. It doesn't lessen my fascination with the humanity of Jesus. Neither does it diminish his genius.

If you are a person of faith, it may feel offensive to you to explore Jesus's genius apart from his divinity. But I believe that we have for too long attributed all that Jesus did, and all that he was, to his divine nature. Other than convincing us of his divinity, I wonder, what can we learn from the Jesus who walked on water, fed thousands with only five fish and two loaves of bread, and healed the sick? Could it be that our fixation on the miraculous has blinded us to the transcendent?

Even when Jesus healed, it always had a deeper intention. He was never showing off. He was trying to change the way we see reality. When he healed a blind person, he spoke of our blindness and insisted that he came to give us sight. It was a metaphor wrapped in the miraculous—a way of getting our attention so we would know there was more going on than met the eye. Like a chicken transfixed on a singular object, we have yet to take our eyes off the spectacular and see the Jesus standing right in front of us.

In the end, he was not crucified for the miracles he performed. He was crucified because he violated the way people saw God, the scriptures, themselves, and the world around them. Jesus was by every definition a heretic. Yet one thing proves to be true over and over again. Once Jesus changes how you see reality, you can never see it the same again.

To fail to see Jesus as a man is to dismiss the complexity of his thinking, the brilliance of his ideas, the power of his character, and the beauty of who he was in full. I hope the pages to follow will change that oversight. Jesus is without question among the world's great geniuses. More than that, I am convinced that Jesus stands alone above all the others.

EVEN NOW I find myself at a curious place in my own spiritual journey. There has always been a great tension in my life from having both deep convictions and endless nagging questions. I am convinced a person can have deep faith and profound doubt at the same time. In fact, I have found that the willingness to question everything—to explore the depth of one's own beliefs and doubts—often leads us to our most profound insights.

Life has a way of sifting through what you really know. When we're young, we're convinced we know everything and we're uncertain about nothing. But as we mature and grow, we become more aware of everything we do not know. Maturity frees you to know less, but to know the less that actually matters. I love having conversations with people whose beliefs have gone through the gauntlet of crisis, uncertainty, and the unknown.

Years ago, a dear friend fell terminally ill with cancer. He felt certain God had told him that he would be healed, and some of his closest friends affirmed his belief. I remember the inner turmoil I felt when he asked me to validate what he believed to be the voice of God guaranteeing his healing. He was someone I loved very much. With every fiber of my being, I wanted to confirm his belief in his imminent healing. I could not.

My silence spoke volumes. The best I could do was affirm that I, too, wanted him to be healed.

A few days later, he took a turn for the worse, and I went to be with him in the final hours before his death. At one point, he took much of the little strength that was left to him to ask me point-blank if he had imposed his hopes on God. There was no need to answer. It was painful to listen as this man I admired confessed that he had mistaken his longing to live as God's will. He apologized for trying to position me to either agree with him or be seen as lacking faith.

It seems strange to me that anyone facing death would feel it was necessary to apologize for believing too much—or at least for believing he knew what he in fact did not. That, of course, is not what I remember of him. He was one of the most noble men I've ever known. What I remember most is how, even at the end of his life, my friend never stopped learning and growing. He faced the ultimate uncertainty. He thought he knew something he did not, and it did not cost him his faith. When he came to the realization the cancer would take his life, it had no effect on his confidence or faith in Jesus. In the end, Jesus was the one thing he knew for certain.

This, more than anything, has been the driving force of my own spiritual journey. What do we really know? I'm not sure if this question should haunt us, inspire us, or drive us. But it's the question that awakens me day after day, and keeps me awake night after night. Why are we here? Is there any meaning to our existence? Is it all an accident? Are we all the products of cause and probability? Can we actually know the things that matter most?

I don't want to know how. I want to know why. I want to know why I am here. I want to know why it matters so much to me. I want to know why I exist. And maybe, if the universe would be so kind, I would love to know *who*: Who is behind all of this?

And what was God thinking when he left us in the dark?

I am confounded by the fact that I do believe—and that I believe so deeply. Frankly, a huge reason I am compelled to believe is because of who I was, who I have become, and who I am still becoming. My high school English literature teacher told me not to bother going to college because I would never make it. Forty years later I am the author of ten books, have won awards as a writer, and have received a doctorate in humane letters. I didn't have a future before my encounter with Jesus. Now, for more than thirty-five years, I have traveled the world and made a living as a futurist consulting with corporations and coaching CEOs, entrepreneurs, and leaders from the business world, professional sports, and higher education.

I am convinced that my life is the outcome of the genius of Jesus, and that the genius of Jesus has as much to do with who he is as it does with who he makes you become. Jesus, as we will discover, carries all the attributes of a genius. He saw the world as no one ever had. He saw human potential where it was imperceivable to others. He elevated the entire definition of what it meant to be human. But his real genius was in making genius transferable. Jesus awakens the genius in everyone and anyone who would trust in his guidance and walk in his steps. If you let Jesus change your mind, he will awaken the genius within you. He will not make you great at physics or music. He will give you new eyes to see the beauty and wonder all around you. He will make you a conduit for the good and the beautiful and the true. He will awaken within you all you need to be fully

alive. What if we are all caterpillars waiting to become but-
terflies? What if the genius of Jesus is that he knows how
to unlock the genius in us all?

It is one thing when genius gives us new music, a new
art form or technology, or a great advancement in science
or medicine. But while genius can give us a better world to
live in, it almost never makes us better, kinder, more com-
passionate, more honorable, more courageous, more humane.

I think of the phrase we often use as an excuse for our
worst behavior: "Well, I'm only human." Our history as a
species is riddled with love and hate, with compassion and
violence, with betrayal and loyalty, with bitterness and forgiveness. All these are equally the human story. The tragedy is that somewhere along the line, the worst expressions
of our nature became the norm and the best of us became
lost in ideals. Religion told us we were all sinners and pen-
ance was our only hope. It mitigated our guilt and shame
but offered no means to restore our humanity. Jesus
changed that narrative. He revealed to us what it looks like
to live fully human through his own life. He then called us
to reclaim our original intention to reflect the image of
God in our humanity.

Jesus applied his genius to the most profound human
dilemmas. Are we as a species actually the worst expres-

sions of ourselves, motivated by ideals that are beyond our reach, or are we most human when we are pursuing those ideals even though we continue to live beneath them? In all his actions—from confronting the use of God's name and the power of organized religion as a means to manipulate and oppress the poor and powerless, to the elegance of summarizing over 613 religious laws into one commandment, to establishing love as the guiding principle of the universe, to reframing power as servanthood—Jesus redefined the core of the human problem as the condition of the human heart. All the problems of the world hinge on this one truth: we have seen the enemy, and he is us. Yet Jesus showed us in himself who we were always meant to be. His life and his teachings force us to confront both the worst and the best within the human spirit, while offering us a way into a new humanity.

If Picasso offered to serve as your mentor with the promise that one day you could paint like him, would you do it? Even if it would take a lifetime?

If Bobby Fischer offered to take you under his wing to transform you into the greatest chess player in the world, but told you it would take you the full span of your life, would you accept?

If Mozart convinced you that if you gave him the next forty years, you could hear the sounds that only he hears in his imagination, and then be able to translate them into music, would it be worth your life?

In Jesus, we have been given this exact kind of invitation. The genius of Jesus is completely transferable. His genius can become yours.

My hope is that as we unwrap the person of Jesus, we will find in him the most astonishing and transformative way to truly live.

CHAPTER TWO

The Prodigy

While there are those whose brilliance emerges later in life, it quite often happens that genius is revealed at a very early age. When a person's genius is undeniable in childhood, we call that person a prodigy.

Wolfgang Amadeus Mozart was only three years old when he first began to play the harpsichord. He composed his first piece of music when he was only five. In the same way, Pablo Picasso expressed his genius for art at an early age. Legend tells us that when he learned to speak as a young boy, the first thing he asked for was a pencil. By the age of nine, Picasso was painting with oils, quickly surpassing the skills of his artist father. He was admitted to the prestigious La Llotja art school in Barcelona and would go on to produce over twenty-two thousand works of art over the span of his life.

In the field of mathematics, Blaise Pascal stands apart as a prodigy. Interestingly enough, Pascal's father felt it was unimportant to teach his children math at an early age. Their education focused on literature and languages rather than mathematics. Yet by the age of twelve, Pascal had secretly invented his own mathematical terminology and independently discovered nearly all the geometric proofs of Euclid. Tragically, Pascal lived a very brief life. He passed away at the age of thirty-nine, but still lived long enough to set himself apart in the fields of mathematics, physics, and philosophy, and to develop what would come to be known as Pascal's wager, which uses probability theory to argue for belief in God.

Prodigies give us the rare opportunity to study genius in its purest and rawest form. If we can understand the origins of genius, we might discover how to replicate it for ourselves. Put another way, we can ask: What does a genius do instinctively that we could begin to do intentionally?

I discovered the critical relationship of the loss of divergent thinking in adulthood and its detrimental impact in every discipline of life while working with universities to develop master's and doctoral programs, consulting with CEOs and entrepreneurs, doing life coaching with professional athletes and sports leagues, and consulting with churches and denominations. According to one study, at least 95 percent of children are divergent thinkers before the age of twelve. In other words, we are naturally inclined to think outside the box. No one needs to teach us to be creative—we are creative by design.

The same study concluded that by the age of twelve 95 percent of us become convergent thinkers—meaning we solve problems through conformity and standardization. This would not be a bad change if it meant we added a new skill to our natural ability for divergent thinking, but in fact, convergent thinking replaced divergent thinking. How is it possible that we begin our lives with a natural inclination to be creative and end our lives with a natural inclination to conform? We are born unique and original, but too many of us die tragically ordinary. We have confused growing up with giving up on our genius.

In their work *Breakpoint and Beyond,* published in 1993, George Land and Beth Jarman detail their work with NASA and later with the Head Start program. In 1968, they had conducted a study to test the creativity, and arguably the genius, of 1,600 children three to five years old, all of whom were enrolled in Head Start. They retested the same children at ten years of age and again at fifteen (a longitudinal study). The results are telling, if not an indictment of our modern educational system.

The proportion of people who scored at the "Genius Level" was, among five-year-olds, 98 percent; among ten-year-olds, 30 percent; among fifteen-year-olds, 12 percent;

and among adults (280,000 of them, with an average age of thirty-one), 2 percent.

"What we have concluded," wrote Land, "is that non-creative behavior is learned."

It may also be argued that genius is clearly intrinsic and that the rarity of genius is a learned behavior. I would go so far as to say that there is genius within us all. The question that demands to be answered is: Where did it go, and what would you be willing to do to reawaken the genius within you?

I've interviewed countless people and taken hundreds of informal surveys while speaking to audiences around the world. When I ask a room, "How many of you would describe yourselves as creative geniuses?" the number of people who answer affirmatively is usually less than 1 percent. Ninety-nine percent of the room consider themselves uncreative, and at best wish they were creative like those they admire.

I usually ask a follow-up question: "How many of you would consider yourselves linguistic savants?" The number who say they do is even less than 1 percent. If the room is full of Americans, most of them speak only English. Who thinks they're a linguistic savant when they only know one language?

But I remind them they all learned to speak one of the

most difficult and complex languages in the world around the age of two. How does an infant learn English if they're not a linguistic savant? I propose to them that if they had moved somewhere else in the world at that age, they would have learned that language just as easily. If they had moved to Tokyo, they would have learned Japanese as if it were their first language. If they had moved to Manila, they would have spoken Tagalog. If they had moved to Rio de Janeiro, they would have spoken Portuguese. And of course, if they had moved to London, they would have learned the Queen's English.

The fact is, every child is a linguistic savant. They may have convinced their brain they only needed to know one language, but their brain was always capable of doing the incredible.

The same is true in other areas of our lives. You had to be taught to color inside the lines. You had to be taught to think inside the box. You had to be taught that the right answers are what make you right. Your natural instinct was to think outside the box. By design you were a divergent thinker. We had to educate the creativity out of you. Before you were twelve, you were a prodigy. I'm not sure who you are now, but I know the potential you were created with.

Who were we as children? Was there a spark of genius

in all of us that we were unaware of, or perhaps have forgotten? Perhaps in finding the genius of Jesus as a child, we can discover our own.

History has proven that genius expressed in childhood does not guarantee success in adulthood. For every child prodigy whose early gifting foreshadowed a life of creative genius, there are ten more whose stories ended early, in either tragedy or underachievement. Far too often, the burden of talent discovered too soon is too heavy for one human to carry. When genius lacks character, it becomes the material of madness.

But what if genius was rooted in the character of the person, in characteristics such as integrity, fidelity, even humility? We most often consider genius as an expression of talent, of "what you do." We rarely think of genius as an expression of essence, or "what you are." Jesus changes the category of genius from talent and intellect to essence and wisdom. This may be the principal reason we forget him when we talk about human genius.

Jesus is quoted as saying that unless we become like children, we will never enter the kingdom of heaven. He also said that his father has hidden from the wise that which he has revealed to little children. Maybe there is more to those teachings than meets the eye. Perhaps the best way to see who we as humans can become is to see ourselves through the eyes of a child.

· · ·

IF YOU'RE A person whose entire life has been shaped by the person of Jesus, it can be frustrating that so little is known about his life from birth until the age of thirty. We know less about the first years of Jesus's life than perhaps any person of equal stature throughout the entirety of human history. If God's intention was for us to live our lives the way Jesus did, you'd think he would have taken care to leave us with far more detail about his first thirty years of life.

The reality is that we can do nothing about the silence we have been left with on the life and person of Jesus. At the same time, it does heighten the importance of the few things we are told about him before he appeared on the scene at the age of thirty.

Luke summarizes all the years from Jesus's birth to ad-olescence in one simple statement: "The child grew up healthy and strong. He was filled with wisdom and God's favor was on him." Then, at the age of twelve, we are fi-nally given our first insight into who Jesus was in his child-hood.

Every year, Luke writes, Jesus and his parents went to Jerusalem for the Passover festival. Passover is a major Jewish holiday that celebrates the exodus of the Israelites from captivity in ancient Egypt. It begins on the fifteenth day of the Hebrew month of Nisan in the spring, and many

Jews observe the holiday for seven days. Historically, it was tradition that those who were able to travel to Jerusalem to celebrate this festival should do so. When Jesus was twelve years old, his family attended the festival as usual. After the celebration, they started home to Nazareth, but Jesus stayed behind in Jerusalem. His parents didn't miss him at first, because they assumed he was among the other travelers. But when he didn't show up in camp that evening, they started looking for him among their relatives and friends. When they still couldn't find him, they went back to Jerusalem to search for him there.

Three days later, they finally discovered him in the Temple, sitting among the religious teachers, listening to them and asking questions. All who heard him were amazed at his understanding.

In those days, the Temple would have been the Hebrew equivalent of the Greek symposium. Israel's most educated and brightest minds gathered there to discuss all the issues of life. They dissected the Torah and discussed the meaning of the Law and the Prophets. They interpreted the teachings of the scriptures. Their conversations spanned subjects from how the Hebrew people must live to the very nature of God himself to such abstract concepts as the existence of eternity and the transcendent nature of humanity. Under normal circumstances, a twelve-year-old entering that space and interrupting such important conversations would have been seen as an act of both insolence and sacrilege. These men would not have taken kindly to the intrusion, which tells you how compelling Jesus must have been from the onset.

His parents didn't know what to think. "Son," his mother asked, "why have you done this to us? Your father and I have been frantic, searching for you everywhere."

"But why did you need to search?" he asked. "Did you not know that I must be in my father's house?"

In this one statement, Jesus reveals that he knew exactly who he was and what he was put here on earth to accomplish. Many of us spend our entire lives trying to figure out who we are and why we are here. Even as a child, Jesus was never lost. He was clear about both his identity and his intention. He always knew where he was and where he was going. Imagine having that level of clarity in your life. It may sound trite, but Jesus could see the real.

Other than this, the Gospels don't say much about Jesus's childhood. After he was discovered at the Temple, he returned to Nazareth with his parents and was obedient to them. Jesus grew in wisdom and in stature and in favor with God and all the people. Luke tells us that his mother stored "all these things" in her heart.

There are apocryphal accounts of Jesus performing miracles early in life that allude to his divinity. In one, young Jesus brings a bird back to life—a foreshadowing of his power over death and the promise of resurrection. I understand the appeal of adding color to Jesus's childhood, especially if it confirms our deeply held beliefs that Jesus was God. But as romantic and magical as these stories may be, they are unnecessary to confirm the prodigious nature of Jesus. The account of him teaching in the Temple is rich with information about the uniqueness of Jesus.

There's so much about this story that points to the dark side of genius. Often, people who are geniuses in one area will neglect the obvious in other areas of everyday life. Think of the billionaire who dies alone, estranged from his ex-wives and emotionally neglected children. Or the hall-of-fame NFL football player who, at forty years old, is living out of his car, having squandered the hundred million dollars he made during his career. Think of the scientist who commits crimes against humanity because he sees people as less valuable than his research. What is obvious to the genius rarely seems obvious to the rest of us. What is obvious to the rest of us is quite often something to which the genius seems strangely oblivious.

At twelve years old, most of us knew that if we disappeared for three days, it would cause our mothers to have a heart attack and would evoke the wrath of our fathers. But Jesus either left without asking his parents' permission, or didn't consider it necessary to at least inform them. (It cannot be overlooked that it took Jesus's parents three days to find their missing son. I think if I had been entrusted with raising the Son of God, I would have paid more careful attention!) When they finally caught up with him, he seemed surprised by Mary's frantic disposition and warranted concern.

In this interaction, Jesus demonstrates many of the common characteristics of a prodigy trying to fit into a world of people who see everything differently than them.

The singular characteristic of a prodigy is that they find their genius early in life. While everyone else is doing the ordinary things of childhood, the prodigy finds their focus. Somehow, even as a child, you know the violin belongs in your hand. You become obsessed. It is less that a prodigy has a talent and more that they have a calling. Others might try to keep them from what they were born to do, but they find their passion and apply their genius to it against all odds. Anything that gets in the way of their singular focus will be discarded and pushed aside.

It is no different with Jesus. Even at twelve years old, he knew exactly what his life was about. He came to restore our humanity by restoring us to the one who created us. Which is why, when Mary demanded an explanation for his absence, he stated the obvious: "Did you not know that I must be in my father's house?" It was as if he were saying,

"If you understood my intention, you would have had no doubt about where to look for me."

You would expect to find Beethoven at a piano. You would expect to find Michelangelo in the Sistine Chapel. If you were searching for Bobby Fischer, you'd find the nearest chess board. The artist always finds his canvas. The genius moves toward her medium like a moth drawn to flame.

Jesus was a prodigy who never lost sight of his genius. While most of us get lost in the complexity of life, young Jesus already had a clarity that is rarely achieved. He knew what the human heart longed for, and he knew how to guide us to its fulfillment. This was his genius. And he never stopped pursuing it as long as he lived.

WHILE THE PRODIGY does not choose his calling, it is up to him to embrace that calling and unleash his genius.

Jesus's purpose was to bring together divinity and humanity. Whatever he went on to accomplish in this world, it would start with this moment in the Temple—the place where God's presence was supposed to dwell. For thousands of years, the most holy of men had spent their lifetimes trying to find the seemingly elusive passage to God. Their forefather Moses had been called a "friend" of God. He spoke to God face-to-face, as one friend speaks to another. The prophets of old knew God and could hear his voice even when he spoke in a whisper. To them, God was an intimate presence, not simply an idea. But by the time Jesus was born, this intimacy had been lost.

When Jesus came to the Temple, it remained the singular place where God had promised to meet people with his presence. Yet four hundred years had passed, and all they knew was silence. The priests and religious leaders had long ago lost any hope that there was something real behind the ritual of religion. God was no longer their friend, but a rumor to be feared. They once talked to God on this sacred ground; now they gathered only to talk about God. They couldn't hear how loudly God had been speaking through four hundred years of silence. Would they even recognize his voice if they actually heard it again?

The Temple was the context for the conversation that Jesus came to have with all of humanity. It was here that God and man were meant to come together in communion. It was here, at the epicenter of religion, that the plot was lost. It was here that the conversation must begin again.

When he entered the Temple, Jesus found himself surrounded by those who were afraid to speak God's name— yet he walked into that place talking about God as his father. The meaning of his statement couldn't have been more clear. The promise of the Temple was fulfilled in the person of Jesus. He was the intersection of heaven and earth. He was the coming together of the creator and the creation. He was God walking among us, flesh and blood.

Where else could Jesus be except in the Temple?

For three days Jesus sat there, deep in conversation with experts on the Torah and the teachers of the Law. These men had spent their entire lives studying the ancient text we know as the scriptures. They were also the stewards of the over 613 laws that had been added to the Law and the Prophets, dictating the Israelites' behavior and everyday lives. We are told that Jesus sat among these great teachers for days, listening to them and asking them questions. It is one thing for a twelve-year-old to have information memorized by rote repetition. It's quite another for him to understand the complexity of the material well enough to ask meaningful questions.

This part of the story has always fascinated me. Luke writes that the experts in the Law were amazed by Jesus's understanding and his answers. But, just before that statement, we were told that he sat among them listening and asking questions. It makes you wonder if Jesus gave any answers at all.

In my experience, the most profound answers are always questions. They are the questions that haunt us, that force us to see truth we would rather avoid. Where is God in our suffering? Is our existence random, or are we here by intention? Why does my soul long for what I do not know? Are we alone in this universe? Is there love, and why is it so elusive? Am I too broken to be healed? Can we know God?

I remember years ago studying the phenomenon of the Baka people, who live in the African rainforests. By the age of twelve, the children of this obscure tribe amass a PhD-level knowledge of botany. What we consider to be prodigious is, for them, simply the skills and knowledge necessary to survive in the most dangerous ecosystem in the world. Children are capable of unimaginable learning, especially when their lives depend on it.

Here, it seems, Jesus knew his life depended on not only knowing the scriptures, but on knowing the God of the scriptures. He found himself in conversation with those who had gained an academic knowledge of the scriptures but were found tragically absent of the wisdom of God. In the Gospel accounts, we learn that these powerful men had used the scriptures to justify racism and bigotry, enforce corruption and greed, and hold the poor and broken hostage by withholding grace from the sinner. They had corrupted the meaning of the Sabbath and used its prohibition against work as a means of withholding compassion from the sick and the poor. These men had used religion to make fools of the sincere, and they thought they were too smart to get caught. Even as a boy, Jesus could see right through them.

Jesus somehow knew what he should not have been able to know. We are later told by the gospel writer John, "But Jesus would not entrust himself to them for he knew all people." He did not need the Temple scholars and religious leaders to tell him about humanity. He knew exactly what was in each person. The way most of us can see the light of the sun, Jesus could see the darkness within the human heart.

After three days, those men who prided themselves on their intellect, expertise, and knowledge of the scriptures found themselves sitting at the feet of this child.

Perhaps it was because Jesus had achieved in his adolescence what most of us find elusive throughout our entire lives, what that very Temple was built to achieve.

He had found oneness with God.

Most of us assume that if we were ever to find God, it would happen at the end of our journey. But for Jesus, the quest could only begin with God. For those listening to him in the Temple, their knowledge of God was second-hand at best—if not, in fact, only a rumor. Jesus found the essence they had been searching for before they had given up their search.

In this encounter, we see the true nature of Jesus's genius: how he engaged people from every walk of life, and how he dealt with controversy, conflict, and opposition. Though the genius of Jesus was divinely inspired, he was constantly expressing it through the little interactions and conflicts that you and I encounter every day.

This is where our exploration of the genius of Jesus has its latent potential. If his divinity is beyond us, I wonder, is his humanity? Or could it be that the purpose of his divine nature is to restore our human nature?

Before we go any further, it might be helpful to ask yourself a few diagnostic questions:

Have you embraced your identity? Do you know who you are?

Have you discovered your intention? Do you know why you've been put on this earth?

Are you endlessly inquisitive? Are you asking the right questions?

Are you expanding the parameters of your intuition? Are you open to the unknown?

Is your essence grounded in intimacy with God? Do you know the God who loves you?

Whatever genius is within you, it was not given to you for your personal benefit but for the good of others. Genius is a form of stewardship. To unlock your genius, you must choose to bear the weight of great responsibility. When Mary asked Jesus why he had gone to the Temple, his answer reflected a nonnegotiable intention: "Did you not know that I must be in my father's house?" He must be there. He must do this. This was not optional. This was his purpose.

There were many things Jesus did not come to do. He did not solve all the world's problems or remove corrupt leaders from their positions. There were many things, too, that Jesus did, but that were not his purpose. He did heal the sick, but he did not heal all the sick. He came to save humanity from itself. He came to do what no one else could do. In this way, all manifestations of genius are the outcome of hyper-focus. Not only does our genius consume us, it defines our intention. In its worst application genius creates a relentless compulsion to our singular passion. Genius creates both focus and blinders.

Which brings me back to that spark of genius all of us had as kids. While you may be convinced there is nothing unique in you, I can assure you of this: there is genius within you of which you may be completely unaware. And your genius is both your responsibility and your stewardship.

I saw genius in my wife, Kim, who was orphaned at the age of eight. When she grew up, she chose to become a third-grade teacher, giving her life to eight-year-olds. In her classroom, she was a creative genius, building castles and ships and creating a world where children could come to love learning and push the bounds of their imaginations. She took the very age she had been when she was abandoned as a child, and made it her mission to create a better world for every eight-year-old child who walked into her classroom. There is genius in that.

I saw genius in my son, Aaron, when he was barely ten years old. The nightclub where our church, Mosaic, met every Sunday was unexpectedly shut down one week by the Los Angeles Police Department. I watched a strange excitement overwhelm him as he asked if he could design the solution to our imminent problem. His young, still developing mind was so pliable and adaptive, he reimagined church that night by creating different stations in a parking lot in downtown LA where people could move from place to place as they experienced the different movements of worship. He organized the crowd into groups of about twenty people per station. At one station, a group gathered to sing and worship. At another station, a group was led in guided prayer. At still another, the scriptures were open and someone gave a brief message. There were approximately six stations in total that night. Every fifteen minutes, a car horn let the groups know it was time to move to the next station. It was a beautiful mosaic. My ten-year-old son had become an experience architect. There is genius in that.

I saw genius in my daughter, Mariah, when she wrote and performed her first song. It was dark and brooding and frankly concerned my wife, Kim, when she heard it. There was so much pain in Mariah's words, the song made us wonder if we had failed in parenting her.

Immediately after the performance, we asked Mariah where in the world the lyrics had come from. She looked at us as if it were so obvious and said, "I've never personally felt that pain. I am writing for the pain of others." Our daughter was a musical empath. Today, her music has been heard by millions around the world. Her lyrics have been translated to such languages as Spanish, Portuguese, Mandarin, Tagalog, and so many more. She gives words to the unspoken longings of the human heart. There is genius in that.

I saw genius in my friend Edwin Arroyave, a son of Colombian immigrants. At seventeen years old, he went to work for a home security company, desperate for a way to take care of his family while his father was incarcerated in federal prison. It was then that he made an unexpected but strategic decision that would change his life. Instead of selling security systems to the rich like everyone else, he focused on those in impoverished communities, who he knew needed security more than anyone.

He began to sell to those who had been completely overlooked by all the experts in his field. As a result, he went from poverty to becoming a self-made millionaire. It makes perfect sense if you look back on it. Of course those who live in areas of higher crime need a way to protect their homes and families. It almost seems strange that no one had thought of it before Edwin. Maybe it was his own struggles and his own background that allowed him to see the world differently. This opportunity had been invisible to everyone else, but Edwin saw it and built an empire. He was an intuitive entrepreneur. There is genius in that.

The genius of Jesus was never rooted in the miracles he performed. Those were the products of his divinity. His genius was always grounded in his character. He saw each moment from eternity. He was not confused about what makes us most alive, what makes us fully human. From the very beginning, he revealed this genius in the questions he asked, in the way he engaged and interacted with those around him, and, ultimately, in his confidence in who he was and why he was put on this earth.

If you choose to embrace the genius of Jesus, you will never see the world the same again. You will never see people the same again. You will never see yourself the same again. The genius of Jesus is grounded in his wisdom, but inseparable from his love.

How that love plays out in everyday life, how that genius is expressed in daily interaction with other human beings—that's the genius we will unfold in the pages to come.

CHAPTER THREE

The Genius of Empathy

I've heard it said that people often gravitate toward the profession that helps them solve their deepest personal problems. I know more than one person who became a therapist because someone in their family or even they themselves had experienced trauma when they were young. I've known others who went to medical school because someone in their family became sick when they were young, and it showed them the importance of healthcare. Even Martin Luther originally became a priest in a desperate attempt to secure his own salvation. Maybe we are all compensating for something when we choose our careers and follow our obsessions.

I suppose I would be one more piece of evidence that this is true. From my earliest memories, I was always found lacking when it came to academics. If you averaged out my grades from first through twelfth grade, I'm pretty certain I would have been a solid D student.

It wasn't that I didn't care. No, it was quite the opposite. At the beginning of each year, I would organize my books and notebooks, sit near the front when possible, and give myself motivational speeches about how this year was going to be different. I walked into every class eager to learn. But, sure as the sun goes down, I would soon find myself falling behind. Honestly, I still don't know how it happened. All I can remember is that I got so bored in class, I would retreat into my imaginary worlds.

It was hard enough to face my obvious lack of intelligence, but what made it worse was that I was surrounded by brilliance. Virtually every one of my relatives in El Salvador grew up to be a doctor. The underachievers in the family were architects, or attorneys, or entrepreneurs. Our recreational sport was chess. In the same way other families value faith and virtue, my family valued intelligence and achievement. You were expected to stand out, to achieve, to rise above the rest. Anything less was unacceptable.

If I had demonstrated talent anywhere else in my childhood—in music, sports, or linguistics—my grades would have been less defining. Or maybe if I had been more naturally social and extroverted, I would have stood out as a natural-born leader. Instead, I was quiet, insecure, awkward, introverted, and detached from the outside world. Every report card was an opportunity to revisit my profound sense of inadequacy. Every sports season was another chance for me to be weighed, measured, and found wanting.

But life has a way of compensating for itself. When you're bad at one thing, you are usually good at another. At least that's the hope. If you're not good academically, then maybe you're a good athlete. If you're not athletic, maybe you compensate by becoming good at math. If you find yourself lacking in both academics and athletics, then look in the mirror—you're probably incredibly attractive. We expect life to have a natural balance. That's why it's frustrating when the tech geek is also the star quarterback, or the math genius is also the brilliant thespian.

While I was clearly unsuited for success by conventional standards, it was that very context that compelled me to discover the power of emotional intelligence. With the same certainty that I could not pass a test, I knew that I could read a room. I could see emotions the way other people saw furniture. I could feel what other people felt, even when they were desperately trying to hide it. I could sense the moment a friend's words hurt another person. I could feel when someone was lying and hiding the truth.

I could take in someone's microexpressions or the subtleties of their speech and feel the hate and love and betrayal and compassion and desire and fear that lay hidden behind them. Words were a secondary language for me, rarely as revealing as this language I had no words for.

It was almost as if I could hear a person's thoughts, a rush of emotion coming from their soul into mine. When I talked to others about this experience or brought up something I'd noticed in an interaction, they would be completely unaware of what I was talking about. What I thought was obvious to everyone in the room was a language everyone spoke but didn't have the capacity to hear. Often this felt less like a superpower and more like a debilitating neurosis. There was so much pain in the world. So much sadness. Some days it felt more than I could bear.

The problem with emotional intelligence is that there is no academic process to validate its existence. "I'm not very good at math, but I feel deeply" will not get you into the best colleges or universities. IQ measures your ability to reason while completely ignoring traits like leadership, creativity, and especially empathy. We live in a culture informed by the Enlightenment, which taught that the highest end of humanity is to think deeply. In pursuit of rationality, we are made to push aside our feelings. This deficit has resulted in a far too narrow view of intelligence and produced many toxic environments, such as corporations where performance and the bottom line overshadow a culture of relational health and shared creativity, to their own long-term detriment.

Frankly, I always saw empathy as a weakness until I discovered Jesus. Growing up as a Latino male, feelings of any kind were seen as unbecoming of a real man. Not only that, the idea of considering others' feelings didn't fit into the highly competitive world of my family. When you are face-to-face with an opponent—whether on the basketball court, in the classroom, or at the office—considering their feelings definitely puts you in a deficit.

In my sixties, I have found places to focus my empathy. I chose to become a writer, knowing that words can change the course of a person's life. My life mission is to be a voice of hope. I know what it feels like to be hopeless. If one sentence can bring a person hope, it's worth the struggle of putting thoughts and feelings to paper.

I also know what it's like to feel alone in the world. A huge part of my motivation for creating Mosaic was to make a community for those who felt like outsiders in the world. I've spent my life studying the phenomenon of genius, motivated by the countless people I've encountered who feel insignificant and inadequate, and are convinced they live at a deficit of talent and intellect and potential. When you're twelve years old, it's hard to see how always being the last one picked for every game is the best thing that could happen to you. My feelings of inadequacy were the environment from which my purpose in life would emerge.

If Jesus reveals one great insight about genius, it is that empathy is the highest form of intelligence. His story is a tale of a relentless love for God and for humanity—an answer to the question "What would it look like if absolute perfect love took on flesh and blood?" What we will discover through the genius of Jesus is that for us to think most deeply, we must allow ourselves to feel most deeply. And this starts by recognizing the genius it takes to care deeply and care well for others.

In the end, we will see that Jesus did not simply come to ensure that we understand God. He came so that we would know that God understands us.

EVERY ENCOUNTER IN the life of Jesus was a study in the power of empathy. On one occasion, a rich young ruler came to Jesus and asked him how he might obtain eternal life. Jesus told him to go sell everything, give his money to the poor, and follow him. We're told that the young man dropped his head and went away sad, because he had great wealth.

In the middle of this story, the disciple Mark adds these words: "Jesus looked at him and loved him." Instead of seeing a selfish, spoiled man who didn't want to part with his money, Jesus viewed him with gentleness and compassion.

Even when he dealt with his adversaries, Jesus's motive was always love. He angered religious leaders by embracing the broken and outcast. He confounded his disciples by commanding them to love their enemies. There were certainly times when Jesus spoke to priests and theologians with such harshness that it must have felt like a weight upon their chests. Yet even these encounters are nuanced studies in both the power of empathy and the subtlety of its genius. Empathy does not always lead you to say what people want to hear, but it does always lead you to say what people need to hear.

Please don't misunderstand me. Empathy doesn't mean always having to say what you're thinking, or making sure people understand your feelings every waking moment of your life. Empathy is driven not by a need to be understood, but by the power of understanding. Empathy is about recognizing what others need in that moment, and having both the wisdom and courage to bring it.

This may seem strange for a pastor to say, but when you stop and truly think about it, it is quite surprising that God would be empathetic.

To be clear, from the oldest Hebrew texts, God is described as a God of compassion and mercy. This description is rooted in an understanding of God's deepest nature. God, we are told in the scriptures, is not only the God who loves, but even more essentially, the God who *is* love. The entire basis for our relationship with God is based on the promise that God is love and that his love is everlasting. All of creation is an expression of love. Love is our intention. It is the reason we exist and the only place where we find our meaning.

Love is the backstory of Jesus as well. In the last chapter, we saw that thousands of years had passed since Moses talked to God face-to-face, like one friend would speak to another. By Jesus's time, God had been reduced to a series of commands, rules, and rituals. While the laws of God remained, the love of God had long been lost and forgotten. All they had left after four hundred years of silence was their memory of God—and they didn't remember him well. They remembered a God of wrath. God remained the judge of humanity, but he was no longer their healer.

We are told in scripture that it was for this very motive that God sent his son into the world. "For God so loved the world" that he sent his son and gave his son on our behalf.

It seems that God has fought over and over again to reestablish us in his love, though we keep replacing his intention with religions built on guilt and shame, judgment and condemnation. God was always a God of love. God always cared. God always grieved over our brokenness and was brokenhearted that we did not know we were lost. God always understood us, knew us, and longed to restore us to himself.

It should not surprise us, then, that if God chose to take on flesh and blood and become one of us, that he would become the perfect manifestation of love. It should not surprise us that the stories of Jesus would be filled with images of compassion, mercy, tenderness, and loving-kindness.

Still, I cannot escape my surprise that God would want to share our feelings. Why would God even care about how I feel or what I am feeling? Why would God feel it necessary, even appropriate, to come down to our level so that he could empathize with us as his creation?

We tend to use words like empathy, compassion, sympathy, and even pity as if they were synonyms, but a more careful examination reveals that they are quite different things. These words, though interconnected, describe distinctly different expressions of love, concern, and human emotional connection. To grasp the genius of Jesus's empathy, it is important for us to understand the differences between these different forms or manifestations of love.

Pity would be the least empathic of these emotions. Its original meaning was rooted in the word "piety." A pious person of well means would be expected to express a level of concern for those less fortunate than themselves. The image that comes readily to mind is that of the poor servant begging their master to have pity on them.

To have pity on someone implies a level of superiority to them. Even though it may be a sincere expression of kindness and motivate genuine acts of altruism, the person showing pity hasn't identified with the object of their kindness. Pity is something you can feel from a distance.

Compassion is the agency of both sympathy and empathy. Compassion goes deeper than pity. It recognizes the "me" in "you." We have compassion for those in whom we see ourselves, and this recognition can lead us to both sympathy and empathy.

We feel sympathy when another person's experience resonates with our own. We may not have had the exact same experience that's causing them distress, but we've felt the emotion enough times to sympathize with them and wish them well. I have heard about husbands who experience sympathetic pain and cravings during their wife's pregnancy. To sympathize we must first recognize what a person is going through and then do our best to resonate with it.

Sympathy is often treated as synonymous with empathy. But though they are both rooted in compassion, they are quite different. A person can feel sympathy without ever translating those emotions to action. Compassion can only be fully expressed through action. When Jesus felt compassion for the multitudes, it drove him to action. It strikes me that compassion causes a mindset shift from the abdication of a problem to the embracing of a problem.

Matthew, Mark, and Luke—all of whom traveled with Jesus—tell us of a time when thousands gathered to hear Jesus and found themselves in a desolate place with little to no food or water. It was late in the day. Jesus's disciples went to him and recommended that he send the masses away to the surrounding countryside and villages to find food and shelter. Their intent was to have the masses fend for themselves. It was the obvious solution to an impending crisis.

Mark notes that Jesus felt great compassion toward the crowd, seeing them like sheep without a shepherd. Instead of accepting the disciples' recommendation, which would have allowed them to abdicate responsibility for the well-being of the multitudes, Jesus instead instructed them to find a way to feed the people who had come to hear his message. You likely know what happens next: Jesus fed the crowd of five thousand with two fish and five loaves.

In this moment, Jesus was not only feeding the hungry, he was teaching his disciples a new mindset. Jesus was moved by compassion, while his disciples were motivated by convenience. Compassion moves you to embrace responsibility, accept challenges, make sacrifices, and take action to serve the good of others. When you see a human problem without compassion, you ignore it. When you see through the eyes of compassion, you are moved to action. Compassion makes you a force for good. Compassion empowers you to live your life with passion.

If compassion moves you to action, empathy is what moves you to understanding. Empathy is the deepest level of knowing. Empathy is more than simply feeling for what someone is going through. Empathy is the ability to stand in someone else's place and see the world from their vantage point. Empathy is the vicarious transference of another person's internal world into your internal world. Empathy at its most profound engagement creates a mystical connection between people. It's the highest form of consciousness. Where there is empathy, there is no separation. Empathy is how love communicates.

Sympathy was never enough for Jesus. His compassion fueled his actions. Jesus cared about people—not just ideas, or beliefs, or morality. What mattered to him was humanity. Jesus understood the human heart in a way that only comes from firsthand knowledge and experience. Jesus understood the depth of the human soul because he cared more deeply about others. His empathy became his source of wisdom. He knew people because he cared about them. And this knowing brought him into conflict with those who were content to live without compassion.

.　.　.

THE TENSION WAS so thick you could cut it with a knife. Jesus had been invited to eat at the house of a prominent Pharisee. He wasn't particularly popular with the religious leaders of his time, so the motive behind the invitation had to be at least a bit suspect. Making it even more suspicious was the fact that the meal took place on the Sabbath. The Pharisees had rules for keeping the Sabbath holy. Rules that allowed them to hide their callous and dark natures behind religious rituals. They knew Jesus, if given the opportunity to do good, would violate the most holy of days. There was no room for mercy on the Sabbath. No room for compassion. No room for good. It was a hypocrisy Jesus could not tolerate.

In recording this moment, Luke notes that Jesus was being "carefully watched." Sure enough, a man suffering from an abnormal swelling of his body appears in front of Jesus. The condition of edema, his most likely diagnosis, is often the result of congestive heart failure, cirrhosis of the liver, or kidney disease. His condition was most likely terminal and exacerbated by severe neglect.

Immediately, Jesus made this man the center of their dinner conversation. He asked the Pharisees and teachers of law who were present a simple question: "Is it lawful to heal on the Sabbath?" This question would have been far more than a legal matter. It's a question about the character of God.

It was, after all, the Sabbath. The most holy of days. What you did on the Sabbath was to reflect how you would live during the week. You rested on the Sabbath to ensure your heart and mind and life were aligned with God's. You remembered God was the source of all you had. If you could not heal on the Sabbath, on the day set apart for God, on what day, exactly, would you do good?

His question had to do with the Law, but it was most certainly a question of intention. What did God intend for you when he established the Sabbath? Was it a way to escape the good he requires you to do? No. It was the way to remind you of the good you must always do.

The religious leaders sitting around the table with Jesus were constantly having endless conversations. They considered themselves the intellectual elite and the premier theologians of their time. They were never too shy or intimidated to give their opinion of what God's actual intention was when writing the scriptures. They were certain they and they alone understood the mind of God. Their status in society was established on their authority to interpret the scriptures.

Yet on this occasion, they remained silent. Jesus asked a simple question, and not one of them could muster a reply. It's amazing how one right question can quickly eliminate an endless number of wrong answers.

If you were thinking like a politician, what Jesus did

next would have been the worst of all possible scenarios. He took hold of the sick man, healed him, and sent him on his way. This was the very thing his enemies were hoping for as they searched for grounds to accuse him. The irony cannot possibly escape us. In this moment when Jesus acted with mercy and compassion, he gave his adversaries grounds to accuse him of violating the Law of God.

What these religious leaders were saying about God was dark and malevolent—that the act of healing a suffering man somehow went against God's character. Jesus exposed that, and it was all revealed in their silence. There is, of course, no way this uninvited guest made it into that room by accident. Jesus's adversaries knew what the noble course of action was. Jesus was so predictable. He would always do what love demands. Jesus would always do the good.

In the awkwardness of their silence, Jesus asked them one more question: "If one of you had a child or even an ox fall into a well on the Sabbath day, will you not immediately pull it out?" This question was more than hypothetical. Of course their principles of withholding help on the Sabbath wouldn't apply to someone they loved. They would not even apply if it were to cost them money or property. Jesus knew that they cared more about an ox than they did about the suffering of a stranger. While Jesus acted out of compassion, they could not even manage to show pity.

From a purely psychological perspective, Jesus's response was nothing short of sheer brilliance. It would have been easy enough for him to detail the religious leaders' concrete legacy of hypocrisy, and enter into the kind of long-winded debate these teachers loved to have. Instead, all he needed were two questions to leave them speechless. Both questions received the same response—silence. With the skill of a surgeon, Jesus cut through layers of intellectual jargon and pretension and left the human heart exposed for all to see. Yet his purpose was not to shame them, but to move them to repentance. His intention, regardless of his audience, was to free every human being from the drudgery of existence and bring them to the fullness of life.

Jesus became a mirror through which they could see themselves. They thought they were angry with Jesus, but it was not Jesus that provoked their anger. It was the darkness of their own hearts. Sometimes the most dangerous thing you can do is to force a person to see themselves clearly. The power of empathy sees into the soul, working with the material of people's hidden motives and intentions.

Jesus had many conflicts like this, which appeared on the surface as a warring of intellect, but were always, in truth, a battle of the human heart. What you could hide from others, and even from yourself, Jesus could see clearly. He exposes your burdens, and then helps you carry them.

THERE IS SO much meaning in the decision for God to become one of us. Why would God become human? Why would he require this kind of intimacy with his creation? What compelled him to come so near to us that he could not remain at a distance? What would compel God to leave the safety of heaven to enter the violence of earth?

You cannot carry the weight of the world from a distance.

It is here where we most beautifully see the genius of Jesus revealed.

For there to be empathy, there must be incarnation. Empathy takes the heart of another person and puts it inside your own soul. Their story becomes your story. Their burdens become your burdens. Their pain becomes your pain. You do not simply feel for them or feel with them; their feelings become your own.

Throughout his life, Jesus connected to the human experience at the deepest level. We see the tenderness and playfulness of Jesus when he allows himself to be surrounded by children. We see his strength, and even his anger, when he drives out the corrupt money changers from the Temple. He experiences the pain of betrayal when Judas sells him out to his enemies, and when his trusted friend Peter denies him three times in his hour of need. At Gethsemane, he struggles with anguish over his future, begging his Father for any other way forward other than the one he must face. At the end, he experiences the pain of feeling alone and abandoned in this world, crying out on a cross, "My God. My God. Why have you forsaken me?"

The only way you can fully empathize with the poor is to have been poor. The only way you can fully understand the isolation of being an outsider in this world is to become an outsider. For Jesus, the only way to fully understand the full weight of our inner turmoil and the suffocating effect of guilt and shame was to bear it all upon himself.

The most profound verse in the scriptures may be the shortest one: "Jesus wept." While I imagine there were many times when Jesus wept, there are only two times recorded in the Bible. Luke tells us of a time when Jesus was so overwhelmed with sorrow for Jerusalem, he wept over the city. Jesus knew what had been lost to that city. They were supposed to be the city of God, pointing the world to the love and hope and life intended by their Creator. Instead, they became a city of corruption and greed and empty religion. The very people who were to lead the world to freedom now used their privilege to hold them captive. They had forgotten who they were. They had forgotten who God was. They would not recognize Jesus as the Messiah because they would not even recognize God if he were standing right in front of them. Jesus understood the implication of their choices. His heart was broken for them.

He could have easily wept for himself, knowing that his love had been rejected. He could have wept that his love was unrequited. But he didn't. His tears were for those whose hearts were hardened and their eyes still dry. Jesus wept for those who did not know they should be crying.

John's gospel records the only other time that we are told Jesus wept. This time, it wasn't for a city full of strangers and adversaries, but for three of his dearest friends.

It seems strange to say that Jesus had friends, but the scriptures make it clear that he did. We know he had followers. We know he had enemies. We know he had fans. A friend, though, was something quite different. A friend implies a relationship beyond obligation. There is no question we need people in our lives. But do we want them in our life, even when we don't need them? There is a sense of mutuality in the word "friendship." A genuine friendship is never one way.

One of Jesus's closest friends was a man named Lazarus. Lazarus was not one of the twelve whom Jesus chose to carry the role of apostle. He was not in that inner circle of three, Peter and John and James. Yet without any official role or position in his new movement, Lazarus had become known as a friend of Jesus.

Lazarus was the brother of Mary and Martha, both of

whom became an integral part of Jesus's life and story. John tells us that Lazarus was sick, and his sisters were deeply distressed. They sent an urgent message to Jesus through messengers: "Lord, the one you love is sick." Lazarus's name did not even need to be mentioned. They knew that Jesus would know whom the message was concerning.

To understand the moment to come, we need to understand the full depth of Jesus's relationship to these people. John carefully makes clear that Jesus loved Lazarus and his sisters. Whatever they did or did not understand about Jesus—his true identity, his mission on earth—there was one thing they knew without question: if they wrote Jesus in their distress, he would come, because he loved them.

The difficulty sometimes is that when we know someone loves us, we often assume that it will assure us of a certain response or course of action. This is especially true when it's God. We hold God's affection hostage to our expectations, especially in our times of need.

Jesus loves Lazarus, and Mary and Martha assume this means he will drop everything and come immediately to his aid. But Jesus does quite the opposite. He seems to downplay the problem, or at least not understand the level of crisis they are facing. Instead of moving with urgency to help the one he loves, he delays for two days before going to Bethany to see his friend. By that time, it's too late. Lazarus is dead.

How often do we assume on God our hopes and desires? If he loves us, he will respond as we expect. If he does not respond as we hope, we see that as evidence that he does not, in reality, care about us or our well-being. Perhaps the most universal question when it comes to God is "Where were you when I needed you most?" It is far easier to conclude that God is indifferent to our struggles than it is to see him standing in our pain.

For those familiar with the story, you know how the crisis resolves. Four days after Lazarus's death, a huge crowd had gathered to grieve the loss of their friend. Some came because of the controversy around Jesus. Returning to Bethany or anywhere else in the region of Judea was not safe for Jesus. It was here that crowds had threatened to stone him. His disciples did everything they could to convince him not to return. Having failed to do so, Thomas responds, with his classic cynicism, "We might as well go so we can die with him."

Jesus returns to Bethany and visits the tomb of his friend. After talking about himself being the resurrection and the life, Jesus calls Lazarus out by name and brings him back from the dead.

But don't focus on the miracle. It's the moment before this that matters for our conversation.

A moment when Jesus stood in their pain.

A moment after which we are told twice how much Jesus loved Lazarus and his sisters.

The moment when he saw them weeping and wailing in their sorrow.

The moment when they could not know what only he knew.

The moment when he could see hope and promise where they saw only despair.

The moment when they felt so overtaken by death, they could not see life standing right in front of them.

The moment when he saw them struggling to believe, yet drowning in their doubt.

When Jesus arrived, Mary ran to him and threw herself at his feet. She cried out with both faith and frustration, "Lord, if you had been here my brother would not have died." How strange that in one declaration, both faith and doubt can equally exist.

In this moment, Jesus was overwhelmed with emotion. Mary was so close to him, he could hear her struggling to breathe. Suddenly he found himself surrounded by those who mourned with her. The sound of their sorrow must have played like the darkest symphony in Jesus's ears. John tells us that Jesus was deeply moved and greatly troubled. There is the implication that he may have been moved to anger.

Anger at what, I wonder.

Anger at death?

Anger at doubt?

Anger at despair?

We will never know. What we do know is that his anger moved him not to indifference, but to action. He asked Mary, "Where have you buried him?" The crowd responded, "Come and see, Lord." I imagine that as the crowd moved forward, pressing against Jesus as he walked toward the tomb, he simply paused for a moment. Then, two words give us a window into eternity—or more specifically, into divinity: "Jesus wept."

In his uniquely poetic way, John interjects the profound into the mundane. Before Jesus confirms his divinity by raising the dead, he shows us his humanity. In moments like these, we want the miraculous, and yet what Jesus gives us is the beauty of being human. It would be much easier to expect a resurrection from God than it would be to expect the empathy of God. Who ever predicted that God would weep? The response from the crowd was instantaneous. They felt the depth of his emotion. "See how he loved him!" they said.

In their literature, the Hebrews have a unique way to make a point. If something has profound importance, if something should not be missed, then the author will say it more than once. It's why Jesus begins so many of his statements by saying "truly, truly," or "verily, verily." It's why Isaiah declares "holy, holy, holy" in describing God. It's why the opening chapter of Genesis repeats six times "and it was good," with the crescendo "and it was very good." The Hebrew language doesn't have a natural way of saying "good," "better," or "best." Repetition is the Hebraic exclamation point.

It is not incidental that John—who is known, by the way, as the apostle of love—surrounds this moment when Jesus wept with declarations of Jesus's love for both the one who died and the ones who had lost the one they loved.

When we think of God, we tend to deify the attributes we covet most. We expect God to be all powerful, and all knowing, and all present. When men desire to be gods, these are the attributes we want most for ourselves. What we seem to have missed is that God is not simply more powerful than us, he is also more caring than us.

When we think of God being all knowing, we instinctively place this characteristic in the realm of intellect. God is the infinite database of information. But the knowledge of God goes deeper than information. It goes to the depth of empathy. God not only knows everything, he feels everything. It is not beneath God to feel. It is not beneath God to care. It is not beneath God to weep.

If you want to be more like Jesus, learn to weep when others weep. If you want to be more like Jesus, allow yourself to feel deeply. By this, I do not mean drowning in the wake of your own emotions, but allowing yourself to be moved by the pain and struggle of others. I always found it odd that when Christians talk about desiring to know the deep things of God, they usually mean growing in their knowledge of the Bible. The deep things of God are never academic; they are always intimate. The deep things of God can only be discovered by love. They can only be known by love. We all want the mind of God, but what we need is the heart of God.

To know God, or his mind, was never intended to be about information, but about intimacy. It's about finding a depth of love that produces compassion, kindness, and the genius of empathy. This was the apostle Paul's desire for all of us when he prayed for the Ephesians "that out of [Christ's] glorious riches he may strengthen you with power through his spirit in your inner being, so that Christ may dwell in your heart through faith. And I pray that you being rooted and established in love, may have power to grasp how wide and long and high and deep is the love of Christ, and to know this love that surpasses knowledge— that you may be filled to the measure of all the fullness of God."

Paul was an intellectual and theologian who found in Jesus a love that surpasses knowledge. He was an unlikely candidate to carry the message of Jesus to the world. He was born and raised by the very cabal that provoked the assassination of Jesus. He was a Hebrew of Hebrews, a distinguished Pharisee who once persecuted the church with the full authority of the Temple. He was also a Roman citizen, which made him a free man, and came from a family with stature and wealth. He was rare in that he was of both the Roman and the Hebrew elite. Yet it was Paul who most powerfully understood the emptiness of possessing knowledge of God without knowing God. For Paul, to know God was to know love and be transformed by it.

We have underestimated the power of love to transform our thinking. Without love, you cannot have the mind of Christ. Without love, the genius of Jesus will always remain elusive to you.

LOVE IS OFTEN seen as primarily an emotion, a soft sentiment that can't match other forms of strength. I hope to convince you that the most profound and powerful expression of love is empathy, and that empathy is the highest form of intelligence.

On one occasion, a paralyzed man was brought before Jesus. Matthew, in recording this event, notes that Jesus saw the faith in the man and responded to him by saying, "Take heart, son; your sins are forgiven." I have a suspicion that this was not why the man's friends brought him. They wanted his body healed, but Jesus healed his soul. And the religious leaders, watching this scene unfold, began to whisper to themselves that Jesus had committed the grave offense of blasphemy.

I love what Matthew writes next. "Knowing their thoughts, Jesus said, 'Why do you entertain evil thoughts in your hearts?'" Matthew would become very familiar with Jesus reading the human heart. Once, when the disciples were walking together, they began to argue about which of them was the greatest. Clearly in the account, none of them said Jesus. Jesus asks them what they had been talking about, and once again we are told, "Jesus, knowing their thoughts . . ." The disciples' response was, not surprisingly, silence.

Jesus was an empath for whom the complexities of the human heart were clear. To put it more simply: Jesus could see us. He would look over the multitudes and find himself overwhelmed. For the broken, he was full of compassion. Toward those who misused God's name to oppress others, he was filled with passionate anger. For those who allowed the temporary things of this world to steal from them the beauty and wonder of the eternal, he felt deep sorrow and love.

Empathy in this form is not only the highest form of intelligence, it may also be our greatest expression of strength. It is no small thing to carry the wounds of another. It takes great strength to feel another person's deepest pains, to carry the weight of their heaviest burdens, and still choose to stand there with them.

This is exactly what Jesus chose to do. God became human, walked among us, and took upon himself the brokenness of all humanity. He allowed himself to carry the weight of all our sin. Within his tears are all the tears shed from the beginning of time until its end. Jesus did not weep for himself. He wept for us all. He chose not to condemn the world but to offer us life.

Perhaps the empathy of Jesus can be best summarized in his invitation, "Come to me, all of you who are weary and heavy burdened, and I will give you rest. Take my yoke upon you and learn from me, for I am gentle and humble in heart, and you will find rest for your souls." But this is more than an invitation to be understood and loved by God; it is an invitation to understand and love like God. It is an invitation to become a healer of humanity's deepest wounds.

It is here that we find the true power of empathy: the power to carry the burdens others cannot carry alone. You may not be able to carry the weight of the world on your shoulders, but perhaps you can carry the weight of someone's burden long enough for them to regain their strength. In my life experience, I have found that perhaps the greatest gift you can give another human being is the gift of being understood. When no one understands you, you are truly alone in the world. But when someone understands you, it makes an incredible difference. When we know we're not alone, we can bear almost any hardship, survive almost any wounding, overcome almost any pain or sorrow.

The power of the empath is that you stand with people in their pain, in their grief, in their fear, in their doubt. You weep when they weep. You laugh when they laugh. You are in rhythm with their soul because you know them as you know yourself.

Some time ago, I was on an airplane headed to Asia or Australia or somewhere far away. It's a long flight from LA to Singapore and Sydney. I would make these flights often before the world changed in 2020. At one point in the flight, I had to run to the washroom, which required me to cross the area where the stewards prepare meals and drinks.

As I walked past one of the flight attendants, I felt something. I don't mean physically. My soul felt something. I can only explain it as a transference of feeling. What I felt was sorrow, coming from her to me.

I didn't know what to do. She was standing stoically without any external signs of emotion. I thought, I am a stranger to her. It's a long flight, and if I say anything it will be awkward for another ten hours. Especially if I'm wrong. No, especially if I'm right. All this was running through my mind in the seconds it took to pass her. And on top of all that, I really had been drinking a lot of water.

Against my better judgment, I stopped and asked, "Are you okay? I sense that something is wrong." Suddenly she broke down crying and began to share with me that she had just found out her husband had cancer. She was devastated. We talked for quite a long time. I asked if I could pray for her and she agreed. (Later, in case you're concerned, I finally made it to the bathroom.)

This is just one of thousands of encounters I could share. Which brings me to a warning that is only fair to give you. If you choose the path of empathy, it will cost you. You will feel all too deeply things you may not want to feel, and you'll lose your ability to hold your own emotions close to your chest. I cannot tell you how many times my kids or my wife, Kim, have called me knowing something was wrong. No matter how far away they are or how long it's been since they've seen me, somehow they have an inside track to my soul. The connection between us spans any distance.

Sometimes the level of connection is uncomfortable, but I am convinced we are all meant to know each other in this way. Empathy is the path to ending the divide between us and the only hope for pulling us together.

Since I began writing this book, our nation has faced four incredible crises. We have lived with a global pandemic that threatened the lives of the most vulnerable. We have also lived through months of quarantine, which has caused massive isolation and disconnection, and endangered those who are most emotionally and psychologically vulnerable. As a result, we have faced an epidemic of fear that has paralyzed millions of people and changed the landscape of human interconnection. With those as our backdrop, the tragic and public murder of George Floyd ignited a firestorm against our country's history of systemic racism. It has been the perfect storm of social unrest. The internet has become a sewer of hate, bias, and misunderstanding.

I have friends on every side of these issues. Many seem incapable of listening to the grievances and pain that inform actions that they deem unacceptable. They see the looting in the streets, but seem blind to the oppression all around them. I am convinced that what has been missing is the ability to empathize. I have been troubled by how many people who profess faith in Jesus have seemed indifferent to the reality of racism—not only in our country, but in the church.

When I was young, I stumbled on the book *Black Like Me* by John Howard Griffin. Griffin was a white journalist from Texas who temporarily darkened his skin so that he could pass as a Black man. For six weeks, he traveled through the racially segregated states of Louisiana, Mississippi, Alabama, Arkansas, and Georgia to explore life from the other side of the color line.

It is interesting that Griffin notes from his travels, "Every fool in error can find a passage of scripture to back him up." He also wrote, "Humanity does not differ in any profound way; there are not essentially different species of human beings. If we could only put ourselves in the shoes of others to see how we would react, then we might become aware of the injustice of discrimination and the tragic inhumanity of every kind of prejudice."

Empathy is needed most in the places we perceive ourselves to be most different from one another. If we could walk in each other's shoes, how would that change us? If we could eliminate the dividing walls that separate us, how would that change humanity as a whole?

Empathy is not about agreement. Empathy cuts through the falseness and finds the truth hidden within all of us. Imagine if instead of seeing only skin deep, we could see straight into each other's souls.

If I could know your heart and, more than that, have my heart transformed by yours—how would that change me? And how would that change in me change the world around me?

Imagine how different the world would be if we could get beyond ourselves and connect to the hearts of those most hurting and alone. If you can imagine this kind of world then perhaps the genius of empathy will be your greatest asset and you will become your world's greatest gift.

Jesus felt our pain and stood with us in it. He lent us his strength so that we might find our healing as well. He never lost sight of our desperate lostness, our need for forgiveness and new life.

Imagine what kind of world we would create if this were our posture as well. A world where we never lose sight of others, because they are now a part of us.

CHAPTER FOUR

The Genius of Power

At age twenty, Alexander III of Macedonia succeeded his father, Philip II, as ruler of what would become one of the largest empires in ancient times. By the age of thirty, he had conquered all the known world. Alexander never knew defeat. His every military exploit ended in victory, and his grasp of culture and philosophy made Greek civilization the envy of the world. He would forever be known as Alexander the Great.

More than three hundred years before Jesus walked this earth, Alexander became history's iconic symbol of greatness. He carried this mantle because he was the personification of power. He stood alone in his prowess as a leader and battlefield commander, and whatever greatness would come after him, in whatever form it would manifest, it would be measured against his standard. The Greek Empire was the aspiration of the Romans, and the legacy of Alexander became the goal of every Caesar who carried that title. The Roman emperor was absolute in his power and claimed for himself not only royalty, but divinity. The Romans ruled ruthlessly, believing that the privilege of conquest was to dominate one's subjects through oppression and force.

Into the context of this Roman world, Jesus was born. A world where greatness was seen as power. A world in which empires built and kingdoms destroyed were proof of your greatness. It was in this world that Jesus, at the end of his life, was given in mockery the title of "king." For centuries the Jews had lived in wait for their Messiah—their deliverer, their Alexander—who God promised would establish his rule and kingdom on earth.

We should not be too harsh on those who expected Jesus to come in this form. It was not unreasonable for them to expect that their Messiah would appear like a new King David to overthrow the Romans through power and force. After all, what is the point of having power if you are still subjected to the rule of an unwanted king? The whole purpose of a deliverer is to stand up to your enemies and set you free.

But it wasn't that Jesus didn't have the power to wage a war; it was that he was fighting a different battle than we had expected. He did not come to deliver us from empires or tyrants, he came to free us from ourselves. That freedom would not be achieved through brute force or the power to rule. It could only be won through the power of humility, service, and sacrifice. Jesus did not replace power with weakness. He showed us a different kind of power altogether. He reframed power as servanthood.

Two thousand years later, our conversations about power have been completely altered by the life of this one man, Jesus. I have worked for years with leaders in the business sector like Ken Blanchard, Patrick Lencioni, and Henry Cloud to establish the Foundation for Servant Leadership—the philosophy that power should be used not to overpower but to empower. I've met CEOs of multibillion-dollar companies who see their legacy not in the wealth they've built, but in their service toward their employees, their customers, and their communities. It's hard to overstate how different this outlook is from the one that has governed society for most of human history.

The concept of servant leadership is profoundly rooted in the genius of Jesus. Jesus saw power as no one before him ever imagined it. Through his words, actions, and sacrifices, the view that with great power comes great privilege began to surrender to the conviction that with great power comes great responsibility.

If the proof of the greatness of an idea is its sustainability and impact, then Jesus's approach to power and freedom might be the most revolutionary idea ever considered.

FOR MOST PEOPLE, the need for power is deeply rooted in a desire for personal freedom and autonomy. For those living in Jesus's time, the stakes were even higher. The Jews had known too many generations of oppression. It seemed that they were always at the mercy of one empire or another.

Which raises a very important question: Can you be free without power? Is there a way to keep your power even when you've lost your freedom?

You cannot underestimate the level of animosity that existed between the Romans and the Jews. To be conquered by anyone would have been difficult enough, but the fact that their conquerors were Romans added insult to injury.

The Romans personified everything the Israelites despised. The Roman emperor believed he was a god, and this alone was unacceptable idolatry. On top of that, the Romans were the epitome of hedonism. Their worship of a pantheon of gods, their culture of indulgence and immorality, their cruelty and oppression of others were all evidence that they were a godless people. They had no respect for the Law of Moses. They had no respect for the Temple, no respect for the sacred. Their imposed presence in the Holy

Land was a reminder for the Jews of why they should have nothing to do with Gentiles.

The Romans allowed the Jews to preserve their culture and their religion as long as they paid their taxes and remained docile and submissive to the empire. Yet there is no dignity in oppression. Living in a continuous totalitarian state leads to an overwhelming sense of powerlessness and resentment. It would eat away at your soul until there is nothing left of you.

The hope of revenge must have always burned deep in the heart of any young, hot-blooded, self-respecting Jew. But the Romans had no tolerance for insurrection or any form of resistance. Any attempt at retaliation would result in immediate execution. Even if you weren't restrained by fear, you knew that any attempt at revenge would be an act of foolishness.

Have you ever started a conversation somewhere in the middle? You knew there was no need to explain the context, because it was already in everyone's mind. This is the way Jesus began his conversation about revenge in the Sermon on the Mount.

When you live in oppression, you tend not to talk about it all the time. It is what it is. You simply talk about life and know that everyone around you understands. The color of your skin is not something you can escape. You don't have to say you are Black. It is always true. I don't always mention that I'm an immigrant when I talk to someone new, but it always shapes my perspective of reality. Some things are always true and relevant whether you mention them or not, or whether you're free to talk about them in the first place. For those who know, the silence says it all. But an outsider could misinterpret that silence, if they don't know any better.

When we read the Bible, we have a way of superimposing our assumption of freedom on the text. We read the scriptures as if the Israelites were like us, living in a democracy free of tyranny. We read the story of Jesus as if he were born free. He was not. He was born into captivity. He was born into oppression. He was born into slavery. Just because your masters and oppressors allow you a measure of freedom or leeway, it doesn't change the reality. Jesus was not born into a free world.

The Hebrews longed for freedom. The bitterness of oppression filled the air they breathed. There is no such thing as a willing slave, content to serve benevolent masters. They begged God for deliverance. They awaited the day when the foot of the Romans would be off their necks. Some dreamed of freedom, others of revenge. To them, violence and revolt were the only path to freedom. This is the world in which Jesus spoke—of all things—about peace.

Almost as if he were answering a question that had not

been asked, he declares, "You have heard that it was said, 'An eye for an eye and a tooth for a tooth.' But I tell you do not resist an evil person."

Then he went even further: "You have heard that it was said, 'Love your neighbor and hate your enemy.' But I tell you, love your enemies and pray for those who persecute you, that you may be children of your father in heaven. He causes his son to rise on the evil and the good, and sends rain on the righteous and the unrighteous. If you love those who love you, what reward will you get? Are not even the tax collectors doing that? And if you greet only your own people what are you doing more than others? Be perfect therefore as your heavenly father is perfect."

Perfection, it seemed, was a reflection of how you treat your enemies.

"An eye for an eye and a tooth for a tooth." I imagine this was something the Hebrews said all the time underneath their breath. Every time a Roman took advantage of an Israelite, they would remember. Every time the hand of oppression stole their dignity, they would whisper this saying to one another. This was the code of the world from which Jesus came. Some might say it remains the central edict of many parts of the world to this day.

When you are the oppressed, revenge requires patience. You hide your hate and bide your time. You convince yourself that revenge is a moral imperative, that there's only one way to preserve your honor, and it's to retaliate in similar fashion.

That, of course, is the problem with hate. It makes us all the same. If the only thing keeping us from acting like those who have power over us is that we are powerless, then we are already just like them.

One of my more painful realizations in studying human psychology has been that far too often, we become the very things we hate. We see this in so many different arenas of human brokenness: when the son of an alcoholic becomes an alcoholic himself, or when a woman whose mother married an abuser seems strangely drawn to abusive men. If someone never should have had power over your past, why allow them to continue to have power over your future?

I'm an immigrant from El Salvador. My heritage is rooted in the long history of violence and oppression that has consumed Latin America for generations. We seem to have only two recurring approaches to government: revolution and dictatorship. With every revolution, there is the promise of freedom. Yet without fail, every revolution brings us a new dictatorship. In time, the oppressed become the oppressors. What history has proven is that we need more than a change of government—we need a change of heart.

It is quite easy to mistake powerlessness for humility. It is easy to convince yourself that you are different from your oppressor when you are powerless to act differently. You can only know who you truly are when you are fully capable of imposing your will on the world around you. Who would you be if you were free to be yourself? Would you be better? Would the world get better?

There is an old adage that's almost universally accepted: "Absolute power corrupts absolutely." While most of human history seems to confirm this, I am convinced this conclusion is wrong. Absolutely wrong. Absolute power does not corrupt absolutely. God has absolute power, and he is incorruptible.

What absolute power does do is far more telling. Absolute power reveals completely. Power gives freedom to what has been hidden within the human heart. Power tells the truth about who we are. Power sets free what has been imprisoned within you.

Jesus seems to have understood this. It's why you can live in a free country and still be held captive by the condition of your soul. He knew there would be a day when Roman oppression ended, yet Israel's need for vengeance would hold its own people captive. Which was why Jesus told the young men who followed him the last thing they wanted to hear: "Instead I tell you: do not take revenge on someone who wronged you."

There was no ambiguity about Jesus's target for this statement. He was speaking to his fellow Jews' hatred for their oppressors. Sure, there would have been deep-seated enmity among the Israelites—especially those who were seen as collaborators with the Romans. This is why there was a particular hatred for tax collectors. I am certain there was also the everyday animosity that happens in our everyday relationships: family conflicts, sibling rivalries, and business dealings that turn contentious. Jesus's instruction would be more than true in each one of those situations. But in this moment, Jesus was speaking specifically about the Romans. To be free of them, he said, you must not become like them.

What Jesus proposed instead was not passive resistance, and certainly not cowardly acquiescence. He offered them a new way to see power and freedom, a way to keep both their power and freedom while still living above the standards set by men who only knew how to abuse and steal.

He said, "If anyone slaps you on the right cheek, let him slap your left cheek too. And if someone threatens to sue you and take your shirt, let him have your coat as well. And if one of the occupation troops forces you to carry his pack one mile, carry it two miles."

I can't even begin to imagine how this advice would've

been received by that audience. They must have thought he was out of his mind. If someone takes from you what they don't deserve, why in the world would you give them more?

Here is the genius of Jesus when dealing with our own sense of powerlessness. You may not always feel free to do less than is being demanded of you, but you're always free to do more. This was true for Jesus, living under an oppressive regime, and it is even more true for us today. You may not be free to show up late for work, but you are free to show up early. You may be legally obligated to pay your taxes, but no one can stop you from being generous. You may feel powerless to change your circumstances, but you always have the power to change your attitude.

When I was a kid, I dreaded Saturdays. It was the day when we were all home as a family, and my mom would have a list of chores that had to be done before we were free to play. I hated being told what to do. I didn't mind the work itself. I just hated the sense of feeling controlled.

I suppose I've always had a rebellious streak in me. I was so keenly aware of my limited power. There would be severe ramifications if I did not do what I was told. I'm not sure how the idea seeped into my mind, but I found the solution to my dilemma and need for freedom: I would wake up hours before the rest of my family and do all the work I expected my mom would ask me to do. I would do it as quietly as possible so that no one would be awakened. I loved the feeling of freedom that came when my mother woke up and saw that there were no chores left for me to do. I rebelled by doing more and doing it without being required. Not to mention that I then had the rest of my Saturday free.

I must confess an overwhelming sense of satisfaction from knowing I was doing all this work without being asked. Early on in my life, I discovered that work done out of freedom is far more fulfilling than work done out of obligation. I could not escape the tasks without consequences. Yet I found my freedom in doing more and doing it of my own free will. This became a principle in my life: do more than expected, and you will always live free.

On one of my trips to South Africa, I had the opportunity to visit Robben Island, the prison that held Nelson Mandela for twenty-seven years. I walked through the narrow halls where Mandela spent the bulk of his adulthood, and I looked into the small room where he was confined. Wrongfully imprisoned, he missed the joy of raising his children, and the dignity of burying both his mother and his eldest son, who was killed in a car accident in 1969. His requests to be allowed to attend the funerals of those he loved were callously denied. That same year, his wife, Winnie, was arrested as well. His letters expressed that know-

The Genius of Power

ing she was free was the only way he ever found himself able to retain a sense of freedom and joy.

In one of his letters, Mandela described how he was forced to sleep naked on the cement floor, which was damp and cold during the rainy season. For thirteen years, he was deprived of even the basic dignity of having pajamas to sleep in. This was a luxury they only gave to the white prisoners, never to those who had the misfortune of being darker skinned. His cell had neither a bed nor plumbing. He was allowed to write and receive a letter once every six months, and allowed to meet with a visitor for thirty minutes only once a year.

Mandela was the victim of a system of injustice and cruelty and outright racism. He remained in prison until 1990, when he was finally released by Frederik Willem de Klerk, the newly elected president of South Africa. On February 11 of that year, Nelson Mandela became a free man—or so it seemed. The world soon discovered that while his lodgings had been a prison, he had actually always been free.

While in prison, he had pursued his law degree. In 1993 he was awarded the Nobel Peace Prize, alongside de Klerk. A year later, Mandela was elected South Africa's first Black president. He chose to use his power not to enact revenge against his white oppressors but to bring his nation together. He chose the power of forgiveness over the chains of hatred and revenge. His life and work have elevated the cause of racial equality and justice across the entire world.

I have great confidence that this is exactly what Jesus was talking about when he described turning the other cheek, giving your coat as well when they take your shirt, and walking a second mile. Never allow anyone else's actions to lead you to be less. Their use of power reveals who they are, and your response to power will reveal who you are. Whatever power you may feel your oppressors have over you, they are powerless when it comes to your character. Only you can choose who you are and who you will become. You can step into a freedom they are incapable of understanding, and stand in your power in such a way that they are powerless to stop you.

There may be nothing more confounding to an oppressor than knowing that those they enslave have a freedom they cannot take away.

LOOK, FULL DISCLOSURE: I'm a fighter. There is a fire that ignites inside me when I see injustice. Jesus's words are not a call for passivity, or even pacifism. In fact, when we understand the context, Jesus is pointing very specifically to strategies prepared for those who choose to war against injustice. If you have the power to change the world for the better, do it. If you are powerless to do anything, Jesus shows you how to regain your power. The proud have never faced a weapon more powerful than humility. Humility is its own strength, though it is often seen as a weakness.

Jesus paints three scenarios in his sermon. "If anyone slaps you on the right cheek, let him slap your left cheek too. And if someone threatens to sue you and take your shirt, let him have your coat as well. And if one of the occupation troops forces you to carry his pack one mile, carry it two miles." He adds to these, "If they take what is yours, do not ask for it back but give it to them."

For those listening, these scenarios would not have been hypothetical. He was describing challenges that confronted them daily. It would not be unexpected for a Roman soldier to try to instigate a conflict with a young Israelite by slapping him in the face. The soldier would only hope that the Hebrew lacked the self-restraint to keep himself from making a fatal mistake.

Jesus's response was not for the weak. When they slap you in the face in an attempt to steal from you your dignity, do not retaliate. Instead, turn the side of your face that he did not slap, and offer it to him. This seems absurd to us today, but it wouldn't have been to the crowd listening to Jesus. The soldier in this scenario would have known exactly what he was doing. He was not allowed to critically injure you without provocation. The only power he had was to diminish you. When you stand there and offer him the other cheek, you communicate that only one of us has been diminished, and it is not me.

One of my favorite films of all time is *Cool Hand Luke,* the classic prison drama starring Paul Newman. It was released in 1967, adapted from a novel written two years earlier by Donn Pearce. This film in many ways was one of my first bibles. It taught me how to deal with my sense of powerlessness. It also taught me how to find an inner power that would give me strength when facing insurmountable odds.

In the movie, Luke is condemned to a Florida prison camp whose rules are far more corrupt than any crime he ever committed. The place is run by a sadistic warden who sees the prisoners as his to toy with and torture. From beatings to being thrown into a sweat box to working as cheap labor, Luke and his fellow prisoners seem less like they're serving out sentences and more like they're enslaved.

Despite all this, Luke seems to have no desire to escape the prison, and at the same time it seems the prison has no effect on his sense of freedom. The most iconic line in the film—"What we have here is a failure to communicate"—is repeated twice: first by the corrupt and cruel warden just after he's beaten Luke, and then at the end of the film by Luke himself, just before he is unjustly executed.

Early in the film, Luke is forced into a boxing match with the largest prisoner in the camp. The prisoner is known as Dragline, and he is a beast. Dragline towers over Luke and all the other convicts. He runs the underground economy of the prison camp and rules the prisoners with an iron fist. The prisoners establish a circle in the yard around the two men, and the warden and guards all watch from a distance. The rules are last man standing.

Of all the things Luke may be, he is definitely not a fighter. The boxing match is never a contest. Dragline beats Luke senseless. Over and over again, Luke is knocked to the ground and nearly unconscious. The few times he actually manages to hit Dragline, his punches have no effect. Yet Luke refuses to give up. Even when it's easier to just stay down and lose the fight, Luke finds a way to get back up.

After a while, the massacre becomes too painful to watch and the prisoners begin to beg Luke to stay down. One by one, they walk away, refusing to stand witness to what's taking place. The warden, who had been sitting on his patio, stands to watch this unexpected scenario. The guards are perplexed by Luke and his resolve.

This scene has always fascinated me. Most men gain respect by proving their dominance over their opponents, but Luke gains respect by taking on the full force of their violence and not allowing it to break him. By the end of the fight, even Dragline, who first took pleasure in beating Luke, implores him to stay down. At one point, Luke can only rise to his knees. Dragline kneels to match him face-to-face and, shaking his head, tells him to stay down. Luke, with the small amount of strength he still has left, manages to whisper a few words—but not of surrender. "You're going to have to kill me," he says, and takes one more swing at the man who has dominated him physically. In the end, Dragline leaves the ring, refusing to continue the fight.

Luke changed the rules. In the most unexpected of ways, he defeats his enemy with sheer courage and the refusal to surrender to power. He is in prison, but they can't make him a prisoner. His freedom is untouchable, even if it ends up costing him his life.

Those who use their power to oppress do not have the luxury of freedom. They are trapped within the small confines of their limited minds and hardened hearts. For them to see someone who is truly free is more than they can bear. There is a strange darkness within the human heart that feels the need to destroy what it does not have or does not know.

Jesus challenged his followers to not let those who abuse their power steal their dignity, or their strength, or their freedom. No one who is genuinely powerful needs to abuse their power and impose it on the powerless. Those who oppress the weak are the weakest of all, which is why only the humble should ever be trusted with power.

It cannot go unsaid that what Jesus called on his followers to do, he did more than us all. If anyone ever turned the other cheek, it was Jesus of Nazareth. It was not weakness that led him to the cross. He had more than enough power to set himself free, but he turned the other cheek and allowed himself to be beaten, mocked, and crucified.

It was his greatest act of strength. Those who used their power to end his life could not diminish him. They were powerless to change who he was and how he chose to live.

Even before then, Jesus chose a life that cost him all the comforts we so often value most. He had no wealth, no home, no security, no family, no position, no title, no means of protection. Yet he made the single most irreversible impact on humanity through both his life and his death. He began a revolution against racism and elitism and sexism that impacts modern culture to this day. He elevated the value and power of kindness and compassion. He integrated holiness with humanitarianism, merging the first commandment with the second. Jesus exposed the lie of loving God without loving people. He established a new ethic for leadership: that to lead is to become the servant of all, that power should be used not to control but to create.

Jesus didn't change the condition of his life, but he changed the course of human history. He reframed our view of power to such an extent that we now expect our leaders to serve the common good. Historically this was not even a consideration of those in power.

If you have the strength to do so, stand firm in whatever injustice you're facing, and be a reminder to your oppressors what true strength really looks like.

AFTER TELLING HIS audience to turn the other cheek, Jesus says that if someone wants to sue you and take your shirt, you should give them your coat as well. The crowd's reaction should be easier for us to imagine, living in a world in which everyone is constantly suing someone else. I live in Los Angeles, which may be the most litigious city in America, if not on the planet. Each year, over a million lawsuits are filed in California. We have buses with giant advertisements for law firms that do nothing but take on one lawsuit after another. The American Tort Reform Foundation listed California as the number one "judicial hellhole" for frivolous lawsuits.

While there are certainly those who need to be defended and who deserve to be compensated for the wrongs done to them, this isn't the fuel of our litigious culture. Lawsuits have moved from a way of protecting the rights of the powerless to a means of making quick cash. Too often, lawsuits are our society's legal version of stealing.

A curious thing about injustice is that it often creates the incubator for justification. The more we believe all corporations and institutions are corrupt, the more justified we feel stealing from them. We conclude that it's all a scam, so we might as well get our own. It is no longer about achieving justice, it's all about getting money. We become a culture of consumers. Enough is never enough. We always want just a little bit more, or maybe a lot more. For years I've taught that we steal because we do not believe we can create. A litigious culture is all about figuring out how to take someone else's money. Greed breeds greed. Corruption breeds corruption.

The Hebrews lived without justice, but among themselves, their mutual oppression did not lead them to greater mutual respect. While the Romans imposed unbearable taxes on the Jews, the Jews, in response, turned on each other. This is why in the Gospels, you find the recurring theme of disdain for tax collectors. Tax collectors were the middlemen between the Roman Empire and the Hebrews. In a real sense, they had sold their souls to the enemy. They were responsible for making sure the Romans received the taxes they demanded from all their subjects, but there was a great deal of leeway in the process. Tax collectors often had unrestrained power, without anyone to monitor their ethics. This became a breeding ground for corruption. Tax collectors would demand far above what the empire required. A significant part of their income came from these amounts. As long as Caesar got what he demanded, they were free to take whatever they wanted. Tax collectors were institutional thieves backed by the power of Rome.

When you feel that what belongs to you has been taken from you, it can easily justify a belief that you might as well take whatever you can from whoever you can. Perhaps the only thing worse than abject poverty is the way in which poverty convinces us to see the world as a system of limited resources, or limited possibilities for bringing about the good.

While putting the finishing touches on this chapter, I received the news of the grand jury investigation into the shooting of Breonna Taylor. Breonna Taylor was a twenty-six-year-old medical technician who lived in Louisville, Kentucky. Three police officers forcibly entered her apartment under a no-knock warrant, issued based on suspected drug activity of her ex-boyfriend Jamarcus Glover. The officers were in civilian clothes, and Breonna's boyfriend, Kenneth Walker, thinking they were intruders, opened fire in self-defense. The police then returned fire, shooting thirty-two rounds. As she left her bedroom for the hallway of her apartment, Breonna was shot six times, and died shortly after.

The case has sparked outrage all around the country, and for good reason. You cannot shoot someone six times by accident. At least that's how I see it.

We learned last month that there would be $12 million in reparations. Today the grand jury decision was announced. Shockingly, there are no indictments at all for her killing. No one will be held accountable for her death. I paused as I was writing this chapter to read a text from a friend who is Black. He said he was both angry and speechless. He wrote, "To hear what the verdict of Breonna Taylor was just makes you wonder if we as Black people will ever be treated as an equal part of the human race."

This man is an educated, successful, former Olympic athlete who owns a home in Beverly Hills, and he feels powerless to bring the change our society so desperately needs. He fears for his sons, that they may one day be mistaken as a threat simply because they are Black. He is a man of peace who is not at all inclined to violence, though he is physically imposing. Still, he feels paralyzed by the injustice he sees happening in the world.

It can happen to us all. We can feel trapped between violence and victimization. Because he has risen above so many hardships and challenges, I am confident he will do so once again.

Too often, though, helplessness creates a poverty of the soul. When you lose faith that there is enough to go around, you become convinced that if you're going to get what you deserve, you must take it from someone else. For someone else to succeed, you must fail. For someone else to have, you must go without. I've known many people who lived in poverty who were incredibly generous, but I have never known anyone with a poverty mentality who practiced generosity. And this mentality has nothing to do with your income level. I've known people with incredible wealth who lacked generosity. As surprising as it may seem, they lived in fear of losing what they had. All the wealth in the world could not free them from clinging fearfully to their money and possessions.

Jesus was speaking into this dilemma. How do you wage war against greed? Greed is most often fueled by a combination of envy and fear. We become driven by greed when we want what is not ours to have, and when we live in fear that we'll never get what we want. If I'm not inclined to steal it from you, I might be clever enough to figure out how to take it from you legally.

Jesus once again attempts to change our thinking about this crisis of the human spirit. How do you fight greed except with generosity? If someone tries to sue you and take your shirt, confuse them completely by giving them your coat as well. Don't fight with them over meaningless things. Rise above them and respond to their greed with a generosity that will confound them.

You can only give a man your coat if you have an abundance mentality. If you are convinced that God is always more generous than you, it becomes easier to be generous with what you have.

. . .

THE FINAL SCENARIO in Jesus's Sermon on the Mount connects directly to the rules of Roman oppression. In those days, a Roman soldier was permitted to demand that a Hebrew subject carry their equipment for up to a mile. Centuries earlier, Cyrus the Great had invented the postal system to carry letters and documents from one place to another throughout the Persian Empire. To make his system work, the soldiers who served as couriers were empowered to force anyone along their journey to carry their heavy backpacks—weighing sixty to seventy pounds, according to some historians—for up to one mile. This would allow their horse to be relieved of the workload and rest while the subject carried their pack.

This practice remained intact during the Roman Empire. Roman soldiers could stop any Jew they came across on their journey and demand that they carry their pack the prescribed one mile. The Roman Road had markers, making it easy to know when this obligation was fulfilled. If a Jew refused to submit to the demand of a Roman soldier, he would be flogged and beaten.

After the first mile came to an end, the soldier would finally release his victim to return the pack to the horse's back. It was only then that the Hebrew was free to leave. For the subject, this journey would have been a two-mile walk of humiliation. The first mile, carrying the pack as if he were not a man but a mule. The second mile, a walk of shame back to where he was first forced to do the work of a slave. Every step would've carried him deeper into an overwhelming sense of powerlessness. The journey was a reminder that his life was not his own and that he was not free to choose his own steps.

Yet even here, Jesus shows us a new path to freedom. When they demand that you carry their pack for one mile, he said, carry it for two. Just when they thought they had broken you by making you walk a mile out of obligation, you have now shown them that you live a life of intention.

In the same way that humility is always more powerful than arrogance and generosity is the great power over greed, servanthood is the singular power that can overcome obligation. Obligation is a false power. Intention is a power that elevates you to your highest freedom.

When you are forced to serve, let serving be your force. Always do more than what is required. Always do more than what is expected. There is no law that is prepared to stop a person who is determined to do more good than expected.

Can you imagine the face of that soldier when he told the subject he was free to go, and the subject instead insisted on carrying the pack a second mile? Can you feel the power in that moment? I can see it now: "No, I'm good. I'm not tired and your horse is clearly not doing well. I cannot fault you for asking for my help. The strength of the Hebrews is well known, if not renowned, across the world."

I don't know what else to call this if not genius. Jesus flips everything upside down. This is tae kwon do in a world of sluggers. It's chess in a universe of checker players. It is the genius of power for the powerless. It is the genius of never losing your power. This is the kind of power that never needs to flex some muscle. This is power so elegant, you never see its force. The wave is never more powerful than the undertow. The power that is unseen is always greater than the power that needs to be seen.

WHAT WOULD YOU do if you found out you had all the power in the universe? What would be your first act to demonstrate your power? John tells us this is exactly the position in which Jesus found himself near the end of his ministry. He reminds us that there came a point when Jesus understood that all power and authority had been given to him. Having known that, he then tied a towel around his waist, grabbed a water basin, and took a knee. As uncomfortable as it made his disciples, Jesus began to wash their feet.

This is what Jesus did with his power. He took the posture of a servant. He chose to die for those who would choose to kill him. He remained faithful to those who would betray him. He offered forgiveness to those who would offer only condemnation. He healed the sick even though it meant that he would forever carry the wounds of his execution. He tied a towel around his waist to serve those who would later claim no ties to him. To serve the world in this way cost him everything. On the cross he looked powerless. Yet the world had never seen such a demonstration of power.

Jesus turned the world upside down when it came to power. His was a genius that eluded all the intellects of his time. How could they have known that power would never know its full force until it was used on behalf of others? How could they have understood that it is not beneath God to serve? That it is exactly like God to serve? If we ever want to know the power of God, we must fully embrace the heart of God. God is the greatest servant who ever lived. There are no feet too dirty for God to wash. There is no life too broken for God to heal. No soul too dark for God to forgive.

Who does this with their power? Who would ever see this as an act of power? Who else but Jesus would make this choice?

This is what power looks like in the hands of God.

This is what power looks like in the hands of a genius.

CHAPTER FIVE

The Genius of Grace

It was 1986, and I was studying for my master's degree while traveling across the country as a speaker. My schedule was often frantic. I spent most days running at a deficit of energy while trying to do far more than I probably should have attempted.

In one of my classes, the professor allowed lots of open conversation and even dissension with his views. For whatever reason, I chose the path of dissension. Quite often I would find myself interjecting or interrupting his lecture to openly disagree with something he had just said. I remember thinking, *I can't believe he's teaching this class*. I wondered how someone with a PhD could be so wrong.

As I look back, I feel a significant amount of embarrassment at my lack of humility, openness, and teachability. I think I saw myself as a defender of the truth. Then one

Tuesday, I rushed into the class—late as always—and something seemed different. All the students were quiet and completely focused on the papers in front of them. A wave of fear passed over me when I realized why. It was the midterm exam.

I felt so confused. *The midterm is on Thursday. Today is Tuesday.* It felt like one of those dreams where you're naked in front of a crowd, only this time, I wasn't asleep. I couldn't contain myself. I groaned out loud and asked—not any one particular student, but the entire class—what was happening. I don't remember if one person answered, or the whole class answered, or the universe answered, but the response was clear and emphatic: midterms.

I turned to my left, where my professor stood, watching the entire scenario. Maybe out of pity, he looked at me and said, "Mr. McManus, please step outside."

He could have humiliated me in front of the class, as I had done to him so many times throughout the year. But he didn't. At least my execution would be in private. At least he would grant me that small kindness.

Still, I worried. Was I being expelled from class? Would he fail me on the spot? This was his opportunity to return the disrespect I'd shown him throughout the year. He should take it, I thought. I certainly deserved it.

The professor was a quiet man. Thoughtful. Introspective. A man of few words and endless deep thoughts. I'll never forget what he said to me that day, as I stood in the dark and dingy hall waiting for the hammer to drop. He took a deep breath, and finally broke the awkward silence.

"Mr. McManus," he said, "there are times in our lives when our only hope is grace. Today is that day for you."

He didn't ask me for an explanation. He told me it was obvious I had confused the dates. I didn't need to justify my incompetence. He simply told me to come back Thursday ready for the midterm.

I'll never forget that moment. A lesser man would have taught me a different lesson. It would have been fair of this professor to teach me the consequences of my arrogance and impertinence, to teach me to have more respect for my superiors. Instead he taught me a different lesson that shapes my life to this very day: There's nothing more powerful than the power of grace. Nothing more beautiful.

I never saw him the same again. His lectures resonated and reverberated in my soul in a way they had never done before. I understood that to sit at his feet and learn was a gift.

GRACE IS A beautiful thing to behold.

When I think of someone being graceful, my memory leaps back to the 1976 Montreal Olympic Games. Nadia

Comăneci stood only five feet four inches tall. She was fourteen years old, competing on the uneven bars for the Romanian gymnastics team with the world's eyes watching her every move. She did what up to then we deemed as impossible, achieving the first perfect score in Olympic history. I remember watching her stand there elegantly as each judge awarded her a 10 out of 10. No one had ever attained a perfect 10; she went on to achieve perfection seven more times under the world's spotlight and against the world's greatest competition.

By the time her career was over, Comăneci had won five Olympic gold medals, redefined her sport, and carved out a permanent place for herself in Olympic history. What I remember most was her smile. It was as if this little girl from Romania was oblivious to the pressure—or at least impervious to it. While the other top gymnasts were fighting to compete, she seemed to be having fun. Perfection seemed like play to her, a source of joy. She was both flawless and effortless. She personified for a generation the very definition of grace.

There are countless more examples from the world of sports. Michael Phelps is the physical antithesis of Nadia Comăneci. He towers at 6 feet 4 inches, weighs 194 pounds, and has a wingspan that makes him look more suited for water than land. When you looked at him, you could not imagine a human being of his size moving at breakneck speed through the water—until he flew from the starting block and did just that. Whether he was swimming freestyle, the backstroke, the butterfly, or the individual medley, Phelps was a wonder to behold. He set world records, winning eight gold medals at the 2008 Beijing Summer Olympics and a total of twenty-eight medals—twenty-three of them gold—by the end of his Olympic career. When Phelps moved through the water, it was poetry in motion. He personified for a generation the definition of greatness.

Grace, by definition, is elegance or beauty of form, manner, motion, or action. It is also the manifestation of favor. This makes "grace" one of those peculiar words that takes on two very distinct meanings depending on the context. Yet there is still a profound connection between those meanings, as we will discover. Grace by any definition is transcendent. Even in the most mundane environments, it evokes wonder. You know grace when you see it. It elevates. It transcends. It carries a touch of the divine. Grace manifests in favor that seems unfair, in works that can only be described as a masterpiece. It is undeniable.

What these athletes have in common is this: They not only made the impossible possible, they made greatness look easy. They made genius look effortless and hard work look like a myth. The endless hours of refining their craft are hidden in the elegance and ease of their performance. Greatness seems second nature to them. While most of us struggle for average, they dance among the gods.

When I watch this gracefulness in action, it always leaves me wondering: Are we to simply be the grateful observers of such grace, or is there a grace we, too, can know? I am grateful to have experienced the wonder of grace when I have needed it most. But can I also become an elegant expression of grace? If I seem to be born with two left feet, how can I become graceful? Can I make being human an act of grace?

I would have given anything to watch Picasso stroke his brush against the canvas or sit in the room observing Einstein as he worked through a mathematical problem. I would have loved to sit down with Leonardo da Vinci and ask how he imagined things he'd never seen, like aquatic vehicles that could dive into the ocean depths or a helicopter that floated like a hummingbird. Imagine sitting at Mozart's side as he worked out which note was next, translating what he heard in his imagination to the keys of the piano. Each of these would be nothing less than experiencing the very definition of grace.

At the same time, so many of those we identify as geniuses have carried other aspects of their personhood that have been less than desirable. They were great at math and terrible at relationships. They were brilliant composers but horrible human beings. Their paintings inspired us with such beauty we could hardly bear it, and their arrogance was virtually unbearable. Yet their genius obligated us to accept them as they were and even, at times, to excuse them for not seeming worthy of the talent given them. I would go as far as to say that we expect genius to come with dysfunction, or arrogance, or even narcissism. After all, how could you be a genius and not be full of yourself?

This is what historians mean when they write about the burden of genius. It is easier, simpler, more accommodating, to see the world as everyone else sees it. Easier to accept the world as it is without question. Easier to belong. Easier to be accepted. Easier to be loved. Perhaps the madness of genius comes in the isolation it brings from the rest of the world. The weight of genius is more than most can bear. I suppose that makes us the lucky ones.

I'm convinced this is one of the reasons why we have for two thousand years missed the genius of Jesus. Jesus does not demonstrate the negative attributes we expect from those with brilliant minds and talent. As we saw earlier, he had friends—close ones—and he treated the lowly as of greatest value. He saw no one as beneath him. His posture toward the humble was always one of humility and kindness.

In this way, Jesus expresses genius in an arena of human development that seems to elude many of history's great figures. His genius can be best seen in how he calls us to relate to one another, how he teaches us to carry the burdens of life with grace.

WE APPEAR MOST graceful when we are at our best and the conditions are most favorable. But it's when we are in the crucible, in the fire, that gracefulness is most needed. I'm reminded of how Bruce Lee famously told his apprentices to "be like water" during the stress of a fight. We are most impressed when someone shows grace under fire.

Jesus spoke often about having grace amid the hard realities of life—most notably in the sayings that have become known as the Beatitudes:

Blessed are the poor in spirit, for theirs is the Kingdom of Heaven.

Blessed are those who mourn, for they will be comforted.

Blessed are the meek, for they will inherit the earth.

Blessed are those who hunger and thirst for righteousness, for they will be filled.

Blessed are the merciful, for they will be shown mercy.

Blessed are the pure in heart, for they will see God.

Blessed are the peacemakers, for they will be called the children of God.

Blessed are those who are persecuted because of righteousness, for theirs is the Kingdom of Heaven.

These are the places and postures where grace is found. They may look easy from a distance, but they are the greatest manifestations of strength. These words are Jesus's way of saying that when the world hardens, become like water.

One incident that stands out to me took place near the end of Jesus's life. In this particular moment, Judas, one of his closest friends and followers, had determined to betray Jesus. When Jesus was praying in a garden outside Jerusalem, Judas arrived with a large crowd armed with swords and clubs. They had been sent by the chief priests and the elders of the people to seize Jesus, and Judas had given them a signal so they would know which man was the one to seize: "The one I kiss is the man, arrest him."

Going at once to Jesus, Judas addressed him with the usual respect and honor, saying, "Greetings, Rabbi." He pressed close to Jesus as an intimate might do, and kissed him on the face.

Jesus's response was so simple, you might miss its power. He said, "Do what you came to do, my friend." In other words, Jesus was not caught by surprise. He knew all along that Judas had come to betray him.

The men with Judas stepped forward and seized Jesus to arrest him. In defense of Jesus, Peter, another of Jesus's disciples, pulled out a sword and swung wildly, striking the servant of the high priest. He cut off the servant's ear in what was either the most extraordinary display of swordsmanship by a fisherman or a fortunate miss as he aimed to behead his adversary. Jesus commanded Peter to put away his sword, kneeled down to recover the man's ear, then pressed it against the victim's head and healed the wound.

All this must have happened in one intense and frenzied instant. But the disciples who recorded this episode could not have missed the implications of what happened. Nothing would have cut more deeply than to be betrayed by the kiss of a confidant. Yet Jesus was not moved to violence, retaliation, or vengeance. Nor was Jesus powerless in this moment. He had the power to heal and the power to destroy. But when Peter initiated violence, Jesus made clear that he came to heal wounds, not inflict them.

Sometimes an act of genius is more than our small minds can comprehend—or perhaps more accurately, more than our souls can absorb. Why would you heal the wound of your enemy and then allow your enemy to wound you with a fatal blow? Why would you choose to still love the very one who betrayed you? Why would you not use force against those who know only hostility? Neither Jesus's accusers nor his followers could make sense of his choices.

There are moments in life that make allowances for the worst of us. Maybe you've lost your job and financial security, and you snap at a friend who doesn't know what's going on. Maybe you shut down emotionally because someone broke your heart. We all face moments like this, when our reactions are forgivable once the context is understood. Yet perhaps it is only grace when it is under fire. The moment either defines us, or we forever define the moment.

Jesus was always bigger than the moment. He never chose to lower himself to the level of those who attempted to bring him down. He always rose above the fray. And from that place, he always calls us to choose the higher way.

He faced the same kinds of circumstances that bring out our bitterness and paralyze us with fear, yet his life was an elegant and beautiful expression of what it means to embody grace. Jesus was poetry in motion.

WHEN WE THINK about the teachings of Jesus, our attention naturally drifts toward what he said about the nature of God. This is no small thing, as Jesus violates the historic view of God as the God of wrath and condemnation and reframes the view of God as a God of grace. But Jesus's view of God also introduced an elegant way of approaching human relationships.

For thousands of years, we humans have considered ourselves righteous by pointing to the faults, missteps, and sins of others. Politicians spend millions running ads that point out their competitors' hypocrisy while concealing their own. Those who are religious hold others to legalisms that even they cannot live up to themselves. Too often we hold each other hostage through guilt and shame.

If God, who has every right to find us guilty, refuses to do so, how can we not forgive one another? If God, who sees everything we've ever done and could easily drown us in our guilt and shame, seeks only to make us whole and give us freedom, how can that not be our intention toward one another?

As with every act of grace, this approach sounds much easier than it is to practice. Giving grace looks easy, but history has revealed that living a life of grace is incredibly rare, and perhaps even impossible. Even in our current environment, we have what is now known as "cancel culture." We ransack the history of every tweet a person has ever written, every statement a public personality has ever made, any joke a comedian has ever delivered, or any mistake a person has ever made in the past, looking for ammunition to end their careers. We do not allow for change, or growth, or simply the imperfection of being human.

Condemning is easy. It's also ugly and inelegant. Grace makes both the giver and the recipient more beautiful.

Grace gives us room to grow, to change, to mature, to repent for a past we are resolved will not define our future. Oh . . . that's important, too. Grace believes in your future.

You would assume that religion would exist so that grace would flow freely, but time and time again the opposite has been shown to be true. While every religion that has ever existed on this earth seems to be built on humanity's need for grace, religion most often uses our need for grace to hold us captive. I learned early on as a Catholic that my eternity was contingent on my conformity. Later, when Baptists led me to a personal faith, I was quickly informed that Jesus was against dancing, drinking, and smoking. There were also several unforgivable sins such as sex before marriage, divorce, and being a Democrat.

Religion dispenses grace as if it were the rarest of commodities, existing only in limited supply. It hoards power by demanding works of us to attain grace—and since the reality is that our need for grace is endless, this ensures that we will always be indebted to the church or temple or mosque or synagogue for its dispensation.

The moment you must work for grace, it is, by definition, no longer grace. It was this very kind of self-righteousness that Jesus came to confront. In a stroke of genius, Jesus came to us to ensure the free flow of grace to anyone who would ask for it.

Early one morning, Jesus appeared at the Temple courts

once again. The people gathered around as he sat down and began to teach. Suddenly the teachers of the Law and the Pharisees threw in front of him a woman who had been caught in an act of adultery. It can be surmised that the woman had been dragged unexpectedly from the bed in which she had slept with a married man and brought to Jesus against her will. She was most likely barely dressed, if not naked.

The religious leaders made her stand before the group that had gathered to hear Jesus teach. John, who records this encounter, tells us that they then posed a dilemma to Jesus: "This woman was caught in an act of adultery. In the Law, Moses commanded that we stone such women. Now what do you say?"

We're told that Jesus bent down and started writing on the ground with his finger. All the while, the accusers kept questioning him, trying to make him condemn the woman standing before him. It is curious that the woman stood there alone in front of Jesus. It's incredibly difficult to commit adultery by yourself. It is far more likely that the man would've been the one who was married. Yet her accusers did not bring the man to be held accountable for his actions.

After seeming to ignore their questions, Jesus finally stood. He then looked toward them and gave them one simple criteria: "Let anyone of you who is without sin be the first to throw a stone at her."

Again, we're told Jesus stooped down and began writing on the ground. Then and only then did her accusers find themselves arrested by their own hypocrisy. When they heard the criteria Jesus laid before them, they began dropping their stones one by one and quietly walking away.

In the end, only Jesus and the woman were left. Jesus, who had been kneeling as he wrote on the ground, stood and look directly at the accused. "Woman, where are they? Has no one condemned you?" Her response was simple and concise. "No one, sir," she answered. Then Jesus declared to her, "Then neither do I condemn you. Go now and leave your life of sin."

From my vantage point, there may be no encounter in the life of Jesus more profound than this one. No moment when grace was so clearly absent and so desperately needed. No moment from his ministry that tells us more about who Jesus was. In one elegant movement he overcame all opposition, all accusations, all condemnation, all shame, and left no evidence of any of it. All that was left was grace.

This moment also tells us so much about ourselves. The crowd thought they had Jesus trapped between a rock and a hard place. Do you fulfill the Law and do what is required, violating the highest law of love in the process? Does the holiness of God trump the grace of God? Would this holy man dishonor God simply to save an undeserving sinner? If Jesus had given her grace, they were ready to condemn him as well.

Jesus's movements were so minimal. His every stroke so at ease. His only effort, we are told, was to write some unknown words in the sand at his feet. It takes so much energy to be judgmental, and giving grace can be even more difficult. Jesus makes it look so easy that the genius of his grace may be too easily overlooked.

In the face of that unconquerable dilemma, he showed that the Law only exists to point us to grace. Or as Paul so succinctly summarized in his letter to the Galatians, "the entire law is fulfilled in this one command: love your neighbor as yourself." The Law is a crutch for those who have not learned to walk in grace.

Linguists have shown that the more experience a culture has with something, the more words they create to describe the nuances of that experience. More words for snow in the Arctic; more words for green in the tropics. In the same way, there is a universe of words that describe grace—kindness, compassion, generosity, empathy, humility, as well as beauty, elegance, and the divine. What if we became experts in the field of grace? What if we made it our language, our essence, our genius?

. . .

IN 2020, I had the unique opportunity to interview Ben Affleck. It wasn't the first time I had been asked to interview a Hollywood A-lister at Mosaic, but it was the first time I had accepted the offer. Using Mosaic as a platform to give celebrities a voice has never been our thing.

That policy may seem counterintuitive. Thirty years ago, we intentionally planted our church in the heart of Hollywood, on the corner of Hollywood Boulevard and La Brea Avenue, and we always knew that our mission was to impact those who are the world's storytellers and creatives. For as long as I can remember, I've believed that whoever tells the best story wins the culture, and for that reason, LA was clearly the epicenter of the future. Still, as important as I understood artists, writers, producers, and directors to be on a global scale, we always wanted Mosaic to be a place where those who work in the industry could explore faith and engage in a deeply personal spiritual journey without ever feeling the church was trying to leverage their fame. Which is exactly why, when my friend Jonathan Bock approached me about interviewing Affleck about his new film, *The Way Back*, I said no.

The film tells the true story of a high school basketball phenom who walked away from the game to spite his father. Drowning in depression, which was exacerbated by an addiction to pills and alcohol, he eventually lost everything: fame, money, and family. Years later, he reluctantly accepts a coaching job at his alma mater and gets one last shot at redemption.

My friend Jonathan knows I am an avid fan of sports and still love to play basketball, so he thought the interview would be a perfect fit for Ben and me. It was a film about second chances, the struggles of addiction, and the hope of recovery, all of which are important themes in our community at Mosaic. "The way back" is something we are all searching for at some point in our journey.

Jonathan was tenacious, to say the least. After multiple noes, he finally sent me a text spelling out reasons why he thought this was the perfect opportunity. He also revealed that Mosaic was the only faith community he and his marketing team were talking to. I found myself agreeing to the interview, just days before it was scheduled to take place.

For me, the tipping point was simple. I felt that an opportunity to have a conversation with Ben Affleck was too good to pass up—mostly because I had concluded that Ben was an atheist, or at the very least adamantly irreligious. I remembered that when he was much younger, he had the leading role in a Kevin Smith movie called *Dogma,* about two fallen angels who find a loophole that would allow them to reenter heaven for a small price: the end of the world. They inadvertently cause an epic battle between good and evil, in which—to add insult to injury to the religious right—an abortion clinic worker is enlisted to save the world. On her quest, she's helped by a stripper, the thirteenth apostle, and Jay and Silent Bob, in this film cast as two foul-mouthed joint-smoking prophets. *Dogma* was about as sacrilegious and anti-Christian as a film could hope to be, and I assumed it reflected Ben's own views about God and the Christian faith.

The Way Back was clearly a parallel to Ben's own story. Over the past twenty years, the actor has lived his extreme highs and lows in the scrutiny of the public eye. He has been celebrated for films like *Argo* and *Good Will Hunting* and ridiculed for others, such as *Gigli* and *Runner Runner.* His own story of addiction, alcoholism, and self-destructive behavior is well known. It's rare to see one person have such extreme success and failure. Even if only for a few moments, I hoped to explore the inner workings of this complex and extraordinary person.

As soon as I agreed to the interview, Ben's publicist began to delineate the boundaries of the conversation. I could not ask the actor about his struggle with addiction. I could not ask him about his personal life. I could not ask him about his family. And I absolutely could not ask him any questions about his personal belief or faith. In short, I couldn't ask him about anything that mattered. All I could talk about was the movie. The strict guidelines almost caused me to give up on the interview, but for some reason I felt I should risk it anyway.

The interview took place at Mosaic one Sunday morning during our gathering. Just before I brought Ben out onstage, I slipped into his makeshift green room to introduce myself and say hello. I had learned in my research that when Ben was thirteen, he had lived in Mexico for a year and that he spoke Spanish fluently. Thinking it could help break the ice, I asked him in Spanish if it was true that he was fluent. Without a second's hesitation, he began speaking Spanish with such ease, it allowed me to see another nuance to his personal history.

When we went onstage, he surprised me by opening up about every subject I was told not to ask about. Without prompting, he began sharing about his personal life. He talked about his family, how his divorce from Jennifer Garner was one of his greatest failures. He talked about his struggle with addiction. He talked about his regrets. He also talked about his faith.

I must admit that it threw me off when he claimed to be a person of faith. He did not claim to have arrived at a particular creed or belief system. He was a seeker, and that seemed for him to be a good place to be. I told him I was a bit disappointed, because I had expected him to be an atheist and thought it would be a great conversation to have on a Sunday morning. But a big reason he considered himself a person of faith, he said, was the idea of grace.

"I find that so powerful," he said. "You know, really moving, and compelling. The idea that God, Jesus, loves us and forgives us. All of us. Everybody. All the people that you know, that you think are great; and all the people that you want to judge and be angry at . . . Really, it's God setting an example for us for how we might be."

He went on to say, "There are people I have a lot of resentments for and are hard for me to forgive, so I carry a grudge. 'They did this to me.' Someone said at church, 'That's like taking poison and hoping someone else will die.' You're holding on to this anger, and that forgiveness is really a gift to the person who is able to forgive . . . To be able to let that go is actually a tremendous gift to the self."

In the end, he said, the hardest person to forgive had been himself. "I regret things that I wouldn't necessarily do differently, but I regret that it happened. I'm a child of divorce. I think it was right for my mother to ask my father to move out when I was eleven. He had a lot of problems. He wasn't able to handle being a father . . . I had a different story in my own marriage, but I think we came to a judicious healthy decision for us. And yet the regret that's there is because I know that I have caused pain to my children. So even choices that you think are okay, 'This is the right positive choice, it's thought out and constructive,' can leave you with a lot of pain and regret. But it comes down to forgiveness. If God can forgive me, maybe I can forgive myself."

What a statement. This Hollywood actor talked about grace the way only a person who has embraced their own brokenness can. He had such affection for the mercy of God, it renewed my own appreciation for a gift so undeserved.

Grace is only needed when it is undeserved. This is the elegance of grace. This is its genius. Jesus left us with a new way of seeing the world. He freed us from the burden of judging each other and condemning ourselves. He lifts us above guilt and shame and shows us a better way to exist. The genius of Jesus enabled him to find the grace for every moment and every person. When we choose to live by grace and give it freely, we, too, step into the genius of grace.

CHAPTER SIX

The Genius of the Good

Around age fourteen, I was introduced to situational ethics, the study of how we apply our values and moral laws in different ways, depending on the circumstances. I was fascinated by the dilemmas we were encouraged to create—how they forced us to consider the priorities through which we lived out our values. If your family was starving and the only way you could feed them was by stealing bread, would it be ethical to steal? If someone came into your house and was going to harm your family, would it be moral to kill them? If you and a group of fellow survivors of a plane wreck were starving, would it be ethical to resort to cannibalism, or would you allow everyone to starve to death?

The tension within situational ethics is that the solution is rarely black and white. Sometimes it's impossible to uphold one of our deeply held values without forsaking another one.

It's easy to believe you would never steal until you're starving to death.

It's easy to believe you would never kill until your life is in danger.

It's easy to believe you would save everyone until you're faced with the reality that you may only be able to save one.

Every day we make decisions that challenge our values, even if we do so unconsciously. When we work long hours, we provide for our families while depriving them of our presence. When we donate to a relief organization in the Congo, we are at the same time choosing to ignore a crisis of equal weight in Bangladesh. Through these decisions and countless others, we establish our sense of what matters in the world. We wouldn't say that we don't care about certain things, but the reality is that life forces us to functionally ignore them.

I see this most clearly in the way different Christians make their political decisions. For many, the singular ethical issue is abortion. If you are pro-life, it's unthinkable and even unethical to vote for a Democrat who is pro-choice. But this posture has led many of us to justify positions and actions that would otherwise violate our own ethical values.

I remember so clearly the public discourse among

Christian leaders concerning President Bill Clinton and his lack of moral character being a disqualification for holding the office of president of the United States. Years later, that standard is no longer used to measure the ethics of supporting President Donald Trump. In fact, some of the very same Christian leaders who opposed Clinton stand eagerly with Trump. For many of my colleagues who are not followers of Christ, this application of situational ethics is profoundly confusing. They don't understand that for many who are pro-life, every other ethical variable is secondary to their decision-making process. This scenario plays out on both sides of the political divide. Most of us are looking for how we can do the most good in a world so often filled with bad options.

The reality is that none of us have time to be engaged in everything that matters—even if it matters to us. One person could spend their entire life trying to give clean water to the villages throughout Africa. For another, the complete focus of their energy might be to bring an end to the global sex trade. Both would be giving themselves to accomplishing a great good in the world. At the same time, they could easily condemn each other for not participating in what they consider the most important humanitarian crisis of our time. I have seen this so many times over the years, leading Mosaic. I cannot count the times people have felt our church should become the platform for their personal calling or passion. In fact, one of our greatest challenges has been finding ways to speak into cultural issues while keeping Jesus at the center of our message.

Whether we realize it or not, real life is all about situational ethics. Each day you make choices not simply between right and wrong, but between the good you will do and the good you will not do.

This is where life gets complicated. Decision-making is so much cleaner when you see the world in black and white. It's even easier when you see the world as the choice between good and evil, as religion has so often done. This belief system—a cosmic war between spiritual forces fighting over the fate of humanity—reduces everything to one of two conclusions: either God did it, or it was the work of Satan. What has been an attempt to bring moral clarity to our decision-making has instead created the context for so much narcissistic and sociopathic behavior. It happened on October 27, 1553, when the theologian John Calvin, as mayor of Geneva's theocracy, had Michael Servetus, who was a physician, theologian, and humanist, burned at the stake for heresy. It happened when thousands of innocents were executed during the Spanish Inquisition.

In our lifetime, people have strapped bombs to their chests, making themselves human weapons in the name of their God. Others have used their beliefs as the justification for racism, oppression, and violence. Each one of them believed they were acting on God's behalf, though history proves them tragically wrong. We must never be so certain of our rightness that we cannot be shown we are wrong. Sometimes we are dead wrong.

Even if we take God out of the equation, the task is still daunting. I've been an environmentally conscious person for over forty years, and it has been so confusing. We proudly went from paper to plastic to save the environment. I was so proud that I was saving trees. Then we learned that saving trees came at the expense of the oceans.

Our lives are full of dilemmas like this. We are materialist if we buy expensive clothes, and propagators of destructive fast fashion if we buy cheap clothes. I recently read an article that you cannot say "Black lives matter" if you are not also an environmentalist. Do we submit to the shelter-at-home social responsibility to fight a pandemic, or do we march to fight against police brutality? Do we stand as patriots or kneel as patriots? Do I buy those jeans if I can't trace back their history? Am I guilty by consumption? Even companies like Nike have felt the ethical dilemma of trying to do global good and their efforts not being good enough.

This extreme view of "good against evil" leaves little room for being human. The burden of having to be perfect is more than the human psyche can bear. And while there is most definitely a battle being waged between good and evil, most of our choices are not made at that crossroad.

This is where the genius of Jesus gives us a new way to wade through the complexity of real life. Jesus does not simply teach us to see the difference between good and evil, or even to choose between right and wrong. He treats those as obvious distinctions. Instead, Jesus teaches us to choose between the right and the *good*. It may seem counterintuitive, but the greatest enemy to doing the most good is living your life always trying to be right.

ONE OF THE interesting techniques in scripture happens when the writer puts together seemingly disconnected events to make the same point. Matthew does this near the middle of his gospel, recording two separate conversations where Jesus dealt with the tension between doing what is right and doing what is good.

The first seems fairly innocuous and almost irrelevant. One afternoon, after Jesus and his disciples had been traveling for a while, they found themselves walking through a field of wheat. The disciples were hungry, so they began to pick the heads of wheat and eat the grain.

It's important to note that this story took place on the Sabbath. When the Pharisees saw this, they pointed out to Jesus that his disciples were violating Sabbath law. You were not allowed to work on the holy day, and in their minds, grabbing wheat from a field was too similar to the work of harvesting grain.

Reverence for the Sabbath was inherent to the Jewish culture. It was on the seventh day that God rested from his work of creating. It was God who established the Sabbath. Yet what had been established as a day of rest had become a day of rules and regulations. Remember, the backdrop to this conversation was that the Hebrews had added around 613 different laws to the ten given to them by Moses—613 laws to make sure you did not offend God.

Since the Pharisees were experts in the Law and the Prophets, Jesus responded by reminding them of a story in the scriptures. He asked if they had ever read what David did when he and his men were hungry. He then reminded them that David went into the Temple and that he and his men ate the bread offered to God, even though it was against the Law. That bread was sacred. Only the priests were allowed to eat it.

Then, since the religious leaders were so determined to uphold the Law, Jesus pressed them further, asking if they had not read in the Law of Moses that every Sabbath, the priests in the Temple break the Sabbath rules by working on that day, yet they're not guilty. How is it possible to not do what is right and still be considered good?

Almost with a tone of condescension, he reminds them that God said, "It is kindness I want, not sacrifices." Then, indicting their entire system of ethics, he concludes with this assessment: "If you really knew what this means, you would not condemn people who are innocent; for the Son of Man is the Lord of the Sabbath."

His point is this: if we're not careful, we will find ourselves living as if the point of life is to avoid doing wrong. That's why laws exist—to keep us from doing the wrong thing. Yet even if you obey every law, it doesn't always mean you've done any good.

From there, Matthew records that Jesus left the wheat field and traveled to a synagogue. This was where the second, seemingly unrelated story took place.

It was still the Sabbath, and the topic of discussion had not changed. Those angered by Jesus's lack of reverence for the Sabbath were looking for a way to accuse him of not doing the right thing. Their attention fell on a man with a paralyzed hand standing outside the synagogue.

The religious leaders saw this man as the perfect object lesson. They asked Jesus the question again, but now from a different angle: "Is it against our law to heal on the Sabbath?"

Jesus began to answer in the way he most often did: by asking a question. He created a scenario that could be easily described as one of situational ethics. "What if one of you has a sheep that falls into a deep hole on the Sabbath? Will you not take hold of it and lift it out?" The question was rhetorical. He knew very well that the religious leaders would not hesitate for a moment to save their own sheep or any possession that had value to them. Then, Jesus stated the obvious: "How much more valuable is a human being than a sheep?"

Jesus turned to the man for whom the religious leaders had no compassion or interest and said, "Stretch out your hand." The man stretched out his hand, and it was completely restored. This was Jesus's way of adding an exclamation point to a statement. He had no patience for those who would hide behind doing what was right to justify not doing the good they could do.

THERE IS ONE undeniable reality you will face if you choose the path of the good: There are those who would rather be right than good. And when you choose to spend your life doing the good, you may find yourself in conflict with those who are certain they are right.

The most direct application of these gospel stories is that you must never allow your religion to keep you from doing good. Religion creates structures that exist to minimize the wrong we do. (Or, to use a more familiar term, religion exists to keep us from sinning.) This is good when the mental and moral structures of religion prevent us from destructive behavior. Too often, though, these rules and regulations become legalisms of our lives and do our thinking for us.

Legalism is one of the lowest forms of thinking exactly

for that reason: it doesn't require thought. Dogmatism and fundamentalism develop when we adhere to principles as incontrovertibly true, without considering conflicting evidence or the opinions of others. Ironically, both religious fundamentalism and socialist liberalism are extreme expressions of dogmatic belief systems.

Early in my faith, I was part of a church that believed dancing was evil. They took this belief so seriously that a young Italian couple was told at one point that their daughter could not dance with her father at her wedding celebration. So much joy and so many beautiful memories lost because of such low-level thinking.

While studying in seminary, my wife, Kim, was supported financially by a couple from her church in Lester, North Carolina. When Kim and I began dating more seriously, they told her they would cut her off financially if she insisted on marrying an immigrant who wasn't white. I am so glad Kim decided to marry down. So much would have been lost to us both if we had listened.

I've met too many sincere Christians who believe that what God wants for them is suffering and who will not allow themselves the freedom to love life. Others are so afraid to risk failure that they never experience the exhilaration of a genuine life of faith. I find it strange that someone can step into the freedom of Jesus and never feel free to enjoy the beauty of the world around them, never feel free to laugh or play or be spontaneous, never feel free to take great risks and great adventures, never feel free to be passionate in love and in life. They live their lives out of obligation and die the slow death of regret and quiet desperation.

The spiritual leaders in the days of Jesus would have spent their entire lives keeping the Sabbath holy. This commitment, though born of noble intention, kept them from seeing that the most sacred thing they could do on that day was to help someone find healing. For Jesus, there was nothing more sacred than doing good.

I have had so many people come to me over the years seeking counsel concerning their life direction. Many have been in their twenties, trying to choose a career and a future. Others have come in their forties and beyond, having built incredible careers but finding themselves unfulfilled. Their crisis of identity was usually more the outgrowth of too many choices, not too few. Especially when they are people of faith, they describe feeling paralyzed by their fear of doing the wrong thing.

My advice to them is rooted in the framework of the good that Jesus taught. I encourage them to ask two questions: What are you good at, and which of those things that you're good at would allow you to do the most good in the world? Whatever the answer is to those questions— that's the good you must do.

Being right is all about you. Doing good is about others. When the right is at war with the good—always choose the good.

Today, it seems there is no limit to the wrong we can do. We destroy the atmosphere by driving to work, destroy ocean life by drinking bottled water, finance child sweatshops by buying clothes, and advance economic inequity by taking a raise. Everything we do seems to have consequences to either our planet or its people. Yet whatever you think about the human condition in its present state, if you believe the scriptures, the status of how we began was quite different. In the beginning, it was all about the good.

Remember earlier when I talked about how the Hebrews used repetition as a way of emphasizing a point? The first instance of a phrase repeated multiple times in the scriptures is found in the first chapter of Genesis, the account of God creating the world. Five times it is recorded that when God finished his work each day, his work was good. On the sixth day, he created humanity—specifically the first man and the first woman. It is only after creating humankind in his image that God changes his description. Instead of simply observing his work as good, it is now described as very good.

Imagine a world in which everything is a work of art and an expression of beauty. Where everything we do, and everything we say, is true. Imagine a world where not only our actions, but our motives, always create life. You don't have to worry about which choice you will make, because there are an endless number of good choices awaiting you. The balance between good and evil is astonishingly leveraged in your direction. That's the world God created for us.

The first command God gave humanity in Genesis was simply "Eat freely." I love this command. In that same chapter, the text says, "The man and the woman were naked and unashamed." It's hard for me to imagine a world in which I can both eat freely and be naked and unashamed—but that's another story. In the middle of a forest teeming with fruit-bearing trees, there was only one tree forbidden to the man and the woman. Other than that, they were free to choose. It was all good.

Most of us feel as if we are fighting our way through a jungle of endless bad choices looking for the one good choice we are supposed to make. When we talk of doing God's will, we speak as if his will is elusive, and perhaps even unattainable. We work from the assumption that every choice we make outside the one choice that is God's will for our life is a wrong choice. No wonder so many of us feel paralyzed, terrified to act. The likelihood our choices will be wrong—or even sinful—is too high to risk. We've come to believe that God's will is like walking on a high wire. Any misstep, and we'll go plummeting to our death.

The Garden of Eden gives us a very different picture of

how God designed us to engage life itself. Every decision Adam and Eve made, save one, would be good. God's assessment of who we were was that we were good. We lost sight of that blessing, and we've been drowning in an ocean of wrong choices ever since. No wonder we created religions with rituals and rules to give us a sense of self-righteousness.

But the genius of Jesus is that he makes the profound painfully obvious. With each of his encounters, he made the right thing to do so clear: do the good that is right in front of you. It may seem simple, but really, it's a stroke of genius.

If you're concerned about sin, try shifting your focus away from what you should stop doing, and instead put your attention on what you should start doing. The best way to stop destructive behavior is to do good. There are so many good things to do—volunteer to be a Big Brother or Big Sister, give one day a week to serve at a food shelter, create community by cooking a meal for new friends, join a Habitat for Humanity build team, and do yourself some good by taking time to exercise, pray, and take long walks to enjoy nature and renew your spirit. If you give your life to creating the good and the beautiful for yourself and others, you will run out of time for destructive behavior. If you make the intention of your life to do all the good you can, you will simply run out of time to worry about the things you once thought you could not change.

For example, having worked with the urban poor for forty years, I know that as a rule it's a bad idea to give homeless people cash. Yet sometimes I do it anyway. It would be so easy to hide behind my principles and ethics of financial stewardship and expertise in working with cultures of addiction, mental illness, and extreme poverty. I know helping one person one time doesn't put a dent in the problem. Yet there have been many times when I just sensed in my gut that it was the right thing to do. Or maybe more specifically, the right thing for *me* to do. Maybe it's a way to ensure my heart doesn't harden behind my logic. Sometimes the right thing to do is the good you can do in that specific moment for the person standing in front of you. Don't overthink it.

Jesus frees us from the endless cycle of worrying about doing the right thing. Our lives were never meant to be about right and wrong, but instead about the good and the beautiful. Instead of asking, "What's the least amount of good I need to do to still be right?" we should ask, "What is the most good I could do with my life?" Look for the good, and know that it is always right to do it. This is what you were created for. This is what you were designed to do.

Living your life for the good will bring an end to the

paralysis of uncertainty. This doesn't mean you will have fewer options. In fact, the contrary will prove most true. When you begin to live your life for the good, you step into a world of endless possibilities. You might feel overwhelmed at first because you'll realize there's so much good to be done. The encouraging thing, though, is that you don't need to be good at everything. Maybe you can't sing, but you're great at accounting. Maybe you're not very organized, but you have endless creative ideas. Maybe you're not a great leader, but you care deeply about those who are hurting. Find your good and get to work. Even if you hypothetically did the wrong good, I don't think you will live with regret that you spent your life doing something that ended up being a waste.

The beautiful thing about choosing between the good is that you create good everywhere you go. You were not created to do all the good that needs to be done. You were not designed to be good at everything. But when you discover what you're good at and begin to give your life completely for that good, it begins to look like genius.

CHAPTER SEVEN

The Genius of the True

When my kids were younger, they accused me of always answering their questions with a question.

One time, my son, Aaron, asked, "Am I a Democrat or a Republican?" I remember running him through a series of ten questions, knowing he would answer five in a way that leaned toward the donkey and the other five in a way that leaned toward the elephant. Frustrated from the lack of clarity, he asked me what it meant that he didn't fall into either camp. I told him it meant he was a free thinker.

When my daughter, Mariah, was eighteen, she was deciding between pursuing a career as a fashion designer at the Fashion Institute of Design & Merchandising or continuing her career as a singer-songwriter. She desperately wanted me to tell her which was the right choice, insisting,

"I don't need your Yoda Zen-master responses. I just need you to tell me what to do." I desperately wanted to tell her. Instead, I just kept asking her questions until she found her own answers.

As strange as it sounds, I rarely told my kids what to do. Instead, I spent most of their lives teaching them to think. I have always been convinced that telling people what to do makes them weaker. I feel the same way about giving people answers rather than guiding them with questions. Answers are like an aqueduct designed to carry your thoughts to a particular destination. The best questions function like a well. The right questions dig deeper and deeper into our own assumptions, values, and motives. Answers are the tools of doctors, while questions are the tools of surgeons. Questions clarify. Questions expose what you are hiding—even from yourself.

If there's one thing I've learned from Jesus, it's this: often, the best answer is the right question. To the frustration of everyone around him, Jesus never seemed to answer the questions he was asked. He always found a way to redirect the conversation. You could easily conclude that Jesus was simply always avoiding the subject. Yet the truth was actually to the contrary: he used questions as a way of cutting straight into the heart of the matter.

In many ways, the question creates the context for the answer. A question can be a catalyst for endless possibilities, or it can be a mechanism used to imprison your mind—to limit the answers that are possible.

Years ago, I was talking with a colleague about the sovereignty of God. He was Reformed in his beliefs about salvation, and determined to convert me. I remember his clear sense of confidence when he asked what, for him, was the defining question: "It's either limited source or limited power." In other words, God is either not trying to save everyone, or incapable of saving everyone. Which one is it?

To be honest, the question felt paralyzing in the moment. I later broached it with my older brother, Alex. When I laid out the two options, he seemed genuinely perplexed that I felt there was a dilemma. He never answered the question. He simply asked, "Why are those the only two options?" What a great question.

In the last chapter, we saw how the questions posed to Jesus often came loaded with dark intentions and forced choices. In these conversations, the religious leaders were afraid to reveal their actual motives. Their singular intent was to discredit Jesus and prove he was not the Messiah, and they thought they could trap him by asking questions they knew would discredit him.

With Jesus, the issue was never the question. The Temple authorities would ask whether it was right to heal on the Sabbath, but the real issue was that Jesus was winning the hearts of the people. If his message of God's unconditional love and acceptance was embraced by the masses, those who controlled the Temple and the synagogues would lose their power over the people. More often than not, their strategy would backfire. Jesus would expose their feigned self-righteousness for what it was—a hardness of heart.

The best way to avoid the real conversation is to control the narrative, but Jesus never allowed his rivals or adversaries to do that. He always somehow knew the question behind the question. Jesus had an unrivaled ability to get to the truth. His questions always worked to reveal, to expose, to expel darkness with his light.

How Jesus dealt with questions is one of the most powerful expressions of his genius.

WE LIVE IN a world where we never let the truth get in the way of the facts. It's amazing the kind of lies we can tell by choosing figures and statistics that work in our favor. When we think of facts, we picture objective information that exists apart from our subjective interpretation. I suppose in an ideal world, that might be true. It certainly is not true in the world in which we live today.

In the months before I learned I had cancer, I knew there was something wrong with me, but I didn't know what. So many doctors were giving me conflicting advice and recommendations. One trusted doctor insisted I should not have a biopsy to determine whether I had cancer. Biopsies, in her medical experience, were more dangerous than helpful. Frankly, this kept me from having a biopsy for several years, not wanting to do something that might cause harm. By the time I went through with a biopsy, the cancer had progressed to stages III and IV.

And that was just the beginning. Once it was determined that I had cancer, medical advice came from every direction. One doctor insisted that the only safe course of action was proton therapy; another told me this was antiquated and ineffective. Another insisted it must be treated with targeted beam radiation, while another told me this was out of the question. One doctor insisted that the only viable approach was to have invasive robotic surgery in hopes that they could cut out the cancer, which had by that point spread beyond my prostate to my bladder and lymph nodes.

These were all good people, experts acting with the best intentions. Yet, in retrospect, at least two of them were completely wrong. I didn't know whose truth to trust.

Who was right? That, for me, was the ultimate question—and determining the right answer was literally a matter of life and death. Too often, discovering what is true is more complicated than it should be.

I think it might be fair to say that the truth is far too precious to be held in the hands of men. To get to the truth—to get to the answers that may save your life—you cannot be afraid to keep asking the right questions. After all, it was Jesus who admonished us, "Ask and it will be given you, seek and you will find, knock and the door will be opened to you."

Perhaps the most infamous question ever asked of Jesus was posed by Pontius Pilate, when he was deciding whether to execute Jesus or set him free. It was clear that Pilate did not want to be placed in this position. He did everything he could to force the Jewish leaders to resolve this issue among themselves, but they needed to involve Pilate. As governor of the territory, he was the only one who had the power to execute Jesus. To do that, he would need to convict Jesus of a crime worthy of death.

The conversation between Pilate and Jesus reads like a sparring match, with neither party conceding much to the other. Pilate asks, "Are you the king of the Jews?" and Jesus ducks the question: "Is that your own idea or did others talk to you about me?" Pilate is clearly annoyed. He's a Roman official, not a Jew, and sees himself as being above their petty disagreements.

Then he asks Jesus, "What is it that you have done?" I find it ironic that the judge in this scenario is asking the alleged lawbreaker to name his crime. Jesus, as he often does, takes up the question without actually answering it. He explains that his kingdom is not of this world—which of course implies that he is a king. He then adds that his servants have not risen to his defense because his kingdom is from another place.

When Pilate asks Jesus again if, in fact, he is a king, Jesus redirects the conversation to the real issue at hand. He explains that the reason he came into the world was to testify to the truth, and that everyone on the side of truth listens to him. This prompts Pilate to ask a singular question that has echoed throughout history: "What is truth?"

There's no way Pilate could have understood the full implication of this question. When Jesus said he came to testify to the truth, his meaning ran much deeper than Pilate's question about whether he was a king. Jesus's point was that he didn't simply come to tell us the truth, or to point us to the truth. Instead, Jesus *was* the truth. What does this ultimately mean, and why should it matter to us? Let's break this down just a bit.

All of us have moments when we are certain we are right, only to discover later that we were wrong. This doesn't mean we were lying. Often we were just mistaken.

My wife is always wrong about directions—and I mean always. But she is never trying to get me lost. She simply doesn't have an internal compass to match her absolute certainty of her rightness. On one occasion, we were heading to pick up dinner at a new favorite restaurant, Din Tai Fung. (Their dumplings are world class, by the way.) As I drove us there, Kim began to tell me which way to turn, even as she questioned how I was getting there. Instead of arguing about the directions, I simply asked her, "Have you ever been there before?" She answered with a contrite and sheepish "No."

Our concept of personal truth is a little like that. It sounds definitive when I speak of "my truth," but my truth may not be an expression of what is true. We are not the source of truth, even when it feels absolutely true. What seems true to us may not lead us where we hope to go.

For truth to exist, there must be a source that is trustworthy. Too often, we're lacking such a source. During the pandemic, for example, one of the most commonly used phrases was "You need to trust the science." But the truth is that science remains silent: scientists speak on behalf of science. And while science is never wrong, scientists are wrong all the time—not because they're trying to deceive, but simply because they were mistaken. There is a gap between the source and the voice. As humans, we perceive the truth and try desperately to embrace it, but we are not the truth itself.

When Jesus says he is the truth, he is saying there is no gap between the source and the voice. He can be trusted completely, because instead of perceiving the truth or learning what is true, he is the singular source of all that is true. He is both the scientist and the science. He is the one who can be trusted. He can never get you lost, because he is the compass and the North Star. Truth exists because God can be trusted.

On that day in Jerusalem, two men stood face-to-face in a battle for truth. One acted as judge, ready to condemn a man he had good reason to believe was innocent. The other stood condemned, though within him there was nothing false. One asked if truth could be known. The other declared that to know him was to know the truth. One treated truth as information to be discovered. The other said truth was the essence of his being.

The answer to Pilate's question "What is truth?" was staring him in the face. Jesus's answer could have easily been, "You're looking at him."

Truth has historically been understood as something you discover. It's something out there in the universe that we find, and then use for some kind of productive end. The genius of Jesus was that he made truth personal. For him, the issue is not whether you are right, but whether you are true. Can you be trusted? Are your intentions clear? In this way, Jesus shifts the conversation about truth from information to essence. If truth does not exist within you, you will be incapable of seeing it around you.

At the beginning of the last century, science was seen as the promise of a better world and more evolved humanity.

We discovered modern medicine, electricity, flight, and so many other advancements. We had at our fingertips the material to create a better world, but by midcentury, the very science that promised us a new utopia brought us Hiroshima and Nagasaki. The truth is a dangerous weapon in the hands of a person who is not true.

We are told by John that God is looking for those who worship him in spirit and in truth. John also records Jesus promising us that when the Spirit of Truth comes, he will guide us into all truth. I wonder if it's possible that we have missed the deeper meaning of these statements. Too many have seen their beliefs and convictions as giving them a monopoly on truth without realizing they have at the same time constrained them from seeing what is true. I have known scientists who were convinced by pastors and parents that believing in Jesus would require them to surrender their commitment to science. They were told that you couldn't believe in dinosaurs *and* in Genesis, in the big bang *and* in the God of all creation. How many thoughtful and intelligent people have we kept from faith because we confused belief with truth? There may be no greater falsehood than pretending to be the guardian of truth.

When Jesus claimed he was the truth, he didn't mean he was a human supercomputer with all the data and all the information held within the universe. The point is not that he wasn't, but that this wasn't what was important to him.

We need to see the subtle difference between the truth and the true. Truth is about accuracy, while being true is about intention. The truth must be first discovered within us before it can be seen in the universe around us. To search for the truth without searching for the true will end as an exercise in futility.

Here's the reality: Throughout your life, you will get facts, data, and information wrong. You will misremember your own past, misjudge the intentions of others, and sometimes simply be wrong about things you were so sure you had right. You will also most likely find yourself rethinking cherished beliefs and deeply held convictions. The genius of Jesus is that he recognized our search for truth is not primarily about trying to be right.

One of the most powerful human experiences happens when you mature to the place where you can know and acknowledge that you were wrong. It is not immoral to be mistaken. It is simply human. And while no one enjoys being wrong, it is quite different than being false. You can be wrong while still searching honestly for the truth. But the truth on the lips of a person who is false will always have the intent to deceive.

This is exactly what was happening at Jesus's trial. Pilate asked his famous question not because he was searching for the truth, but because he was running from it. He was caught up in the politics of his day, and the implication of who Jesus was had a direct bearing on his own position and power. He didn't want to know if Jesus was innocent. He wanted to wash his hands of all responsibility. Pilate could not see the truth because it was not within him. Too often, we mask our fear of the truth by asking questions we believe no one can answer.

Years ago, I found myself in a heated debate with a brilliant atheist at a weekly Q&A that we hosted at Mosaic. He was angry at God for the hypocrisy he experienced growing up in church. There were probably two hundred people in the room, but this man was the only one asking questions. It's not that no one else had anything to say—he simply did not allow anyone else the opportunity to join the conversation. Each time I answered his question, he would come at me with another, without stopping to reflect.

For an atheist to be angry at God always seems like such a strange thing to me. By the man's third or fourth question, I realized I wasn't making any progress. And I sensed his questions were disingenuous. His questions were not for the purpose of discovery, but to prove his intellectual superiority. I am more than happy to admit that many people are way smarter than me, but that wasn't the point of this gathering.

Just before the man posed what would be his last question, I asked him to pause. "I will answer one more question," I said, "if it is the question that keeps you from trusting God with your life." I challenged him to ask me the question that if I answered it well, he would acknowledge his need for God and open his soul to the invitation of Jesus.

There passed what seemed an eternity of silence. The man seemed to find himself at an unexpected crossroad. He was loaded with questions that had kept him from faith, but unprepared to voice the one question that would allow him to believe. He finally broke the silence by asking me for a rain check. He said that question was too important to ask on such short notice. He asked if he could think about it for a week and return the next week to continue the conversation. I said, "Of course. Take your time and find the questions that will lead you to the answers you seek."

He never did come back. Sometimes the weight of that ultimate question is more than we are ready to bear. I hope that there came a day when he found the courage to ask it.

You would think the truth would make you more dogmatic, but in fact, the opposite is true. The person who genuinely searches for truth will always have an open mind and an open heart. When someone asked Jesus when his father would bring the culmination of the age, his answer was, quite simply, "I don't know." When we hold too tightly to the truths that give us comfort, we are in danger of choosing the security of a lie.

I have many friends who consider themselves atheists, and I've realized over the years that not all atheists are the same. When someone self-identifies as an atheist, I will always ask them up front to clarify what they mean by that term. "Are you the kind of atheist who would love to know there was a God if he did exist, or the kind of atheist who wouldn't want to know if they were wrong?" I think this is a helpful exercise for all of us, regardless of how we identify.

The responses I've received over the years are quite varied. I've had atheists tell me that while they don't believe there's empirical evidence for the existence of God, they would love to know if they were wrong. They admit that they don't know for sure that there is no God; it is simply their most honest conclusion. They understand that their convictions are based on an interpretation of data, and they are open to new information.

Others have responded to my question by telling me they know there is no God. They have no doubt that God doesn't exist and are absolutely convinced that those who disagree are delusional. They see themselves as being supremely rational and believe that their conclusions are not interpretations of facts or shaded by subjectivity. Their underlying conclusion: What they know is all that can be known.

I remember one guy just flat out told me, "I'm the kind of atheist who doesn't care." For him, the possibility of God seemed invasive and intrusive to his life. Intrusive in the sense that if God has consciousness and is more than a universal energy, then he probably has intentions and expectations for us as his creation. Even worse, he may be a moral God, who will hold us accountable for how we treat each other. Those assumptions aren't wrong. If there is a God, and he created us in his image, then our lives have both intention and responsibility.

But that's the point. The genius of Jesus is that he does not allow us to objectify truth, viewing it as mere intellectual knowledge that we can treat however we please. The only truth that really matters is the truth that changes us. If the truth doesn't make you true, then it's a lie.

This thought should be sobering to those of us who are Christians.

If we have been transformed by a loving God, shouldn't we become more loving?

If we have experienced forgiveness, shouldn't we become more forgiving?

If we have come to know the source of hope, shouldn't we become more hopeful?

If we have been re-created by the Creator who is the source of all creativity, shouldn't we become more creative?

If we belong to the one who is good and beautiful and

true, shouldn't this reflect who we are as well? Are we not the singular proof that remains of whether what Jesus claimed is true?

It is undeniable that the universe has intention. Even those who do not believe in God advocate for our moral responsibility when it comes to issues like inequality or climate change. It doesn't take a belief in God, or a belief that humans have much control over global warming, to recognize that humans have damaged the oceans, polluted the atmosphere, and harmed countless species that share this planet with us.

For this planet to sustain life, every plant, ecosystem, and creature must do what it was designed to do. Human existence is dependent on the intention behind every detail of creation. Yet we are the singular species on this planet that has convinced itself it exists without intention. We live in this extraordinary ecosystem, in which everything is interdependent and interconnected, yet our consciousness has us convinced that we are outside nature, not within it. The scriptures tell us that all creation declares the glory of God. That includes us—or at least it's supposed to.

The problem is not that science points away from God. The problem is that *we* point away from God. It appears that the universe is pointing in the wrong direction, but it is humanity that is going in the wrong direction. Maybe it's hard to believe that creation has what humanity is missing.

Every morning I wake up confident that the air I breathe is what my lungs will need.

Every morning I take for granted that gravity will keep everything in its place and, at the same time, not crush me under its weight.

Every morning I wake up not the slightest bit concerned that the distance between the sun and the Earth won't remain exactly as it should.

Every morning I act as if I'm standing on solid ground while Earth is in constant motion, floating in the vastness of space.

Every morning I live as if the universe can be trusted.

It seems the only question that remains is, "Can I?"

Can I be trusted? Am I true?

The question becomes more universal as we struggle through this thing called life. Life cannot be survived without at least a minimal level of trust. Every day we are required to put our trust in strangers whom we do not know and may never see. We eat in restaurants, fly on planes, and take vitamins designed and packaged by corporations whose principal goal is profit. And this is just the level of trust that's required to make it through the day. Ironically, if we really did know these people we depend on, or even see them, we might choose not to trust them.

As you venture deeper into human relationships, trust becomes more essential. You cannot have intimacy without trust. You cannot have friendships without trust. You can't even have economic stability without trust. We put our money in banks that have often misused it. You read a book by an author you do not know, and you decide, consciously or unconsciously, whether to believe what they're saying. There is no arena of human experience where trust is not required. From love to friendship to marriage to business to governments, everything humans build is built on trust.

But it goes deeper than that. Human beings are designed to live in truth. Anything less than the truth is toxic to the human spirit. There are no good lies, even when they are well intended. When a business partner hides the financial struggles of his company "just until I can fix it," he not only loses the help of his partners, he loses their confidence and trust. When a doctor tells me what I want to hear, he does so at the expense of telling me the truth I need to hear. You cannot move to health without the truth.

We have reduced the conversations about truth to moralizing about the consequences of lying. But the point is not simply that lying is wrong; it's that lying is toxic. When we allow ourselves to become false, we are poisoning our souls. This is about so much more than telling the truth. It is about being trustworthy, because the truth dwells within you.

Perhaps the most important question we can ask ourselves is, "Am I true?" What is my intention toward others? Do I only wish good toward others, even those who wish me harm? Am I true to my word? More than that, are my words and my actions so aligned that I live in truth?

When you are true, you are transparent. People can see right through you. It is because you have nothing to hide. I think it was Mark Twain who said, "If you tell the truth, you don't have to remember anything." The more you lie, the more you have to remember what you said.

Due to a particular neurological condition, I have gaps in my memory. I either remember everything to an eidetic level, or I remember nothing. I learned early in life that my brain left me no option but to always tell the truth. The more you lie, the more you have to remember. If you always tell the truth, you don't have to remember anything. I may be wrong—and I am often. But I won't lie to you. I hope to be like Nathaniel, whom Jesus saw under the fig tree and said, "Here is a person with no guile"—nothing false in his soul.

I DO NOT think it is incidental that the two most significant names for the Evil One are Devil and Satan. Both names mean something along the lines of "slanderer," "liar," "deceiver," and "adversary." Evil is at war with truth, at war with the source of truth, and at war with all who are true. The personification of evil is the one who has no truth in them. Or more poignantly, the one who cannot be trusted.

In the same way that our lungs are designed to inhale oxygen and exhale carbon dioxide our souls are designed to inhale and exhale truth. Truth is the natural habitat of the human species, the place where we live best. When we choose to step into the truth regardless of the consequences or outcome, it feels like breathing fresh air into our soul.

I look back over my life and realize that I have spent my life searching for truth. I have spent my years exploring Catholicism, mysticism, Buddhism, and Greek and Western philosophy, and have read countless books hoping to find my way to truth. But I wasn't searching for facts. I was searching for me. What drove me was not the hope that truth could be found, but the hope that I could ever become true.

I cannot fully express how it affected me to discover that the dad who raised me was not my biological father. I cannot overstate how confusing it was to be an immigrant from El Salvador whose last name was McManus. The name came from my stepfather, but when I was around fourteen, I learned that it was an alias. It took Jesus to help me understand that truth exists because God can be trusted.

There were so many truths that would be unveiled over the years. Yet in the end, none of the things that were hidden had the negative effects my parents had anticipated.

Every time I was given the gift of the truth, the truth set me free. It was the well-intended withholding of the truth that ended up being toxic to my soul.

Maybe that's why therapy is so powerful. It's a place where we can finally face our truth. The truth, no matter how painful, is our only path to healing and wholeness. It appears Jesus knew this all along. His genius was that he moved truth from the abstract to the intimate. Jesus made truth personal.

If you are searching for the truth, your search begins with becoming a person of truth. The quest for truth must always begin with your inner world. It's a journey that begins and ends with Jesus. To search for truth is to choose the way of Jesus. When you know him and follow in his steps, you not only begin a journey of truth, but find freedom as he makes you a person of truth.

CHAPTER EIGHT

The Genius of the Beautiful

I've always wondered, do geniuses ever truly know the full measure of what they've created?

Did Leonardo da Vinci understand that for generations to come, multitudes would stand before the *Mona Lisa* and gaze into her eyes, lost in her beauty? When Michael Jordan exploded from the free-throw line for a dunk no one had ever imagined possible, did he have even the slightest clue it would become an iconic moment for the game of basketball and the symbol of one of the world's most successful sports brands? Did Einstein know that he would be forever identified with $E = mc^2$?

Few remember the names Perugino, Pinturicchio, Ghirlandaio, Rosselli. All were leading Renaissance artists commissioned to paint the walls of the Sistine Chapel. Years later, an artist named Michelangelo painted the ceiling.

Why is it that he and he alone is remembered as the genius behind this work of art?

The irony is that Michelangelo did not want this commission. He was a sculptor, not a painter. He did not prefer the brush. He would have rather made the statue of David than paint a ceiling, yet he accepted the task and used it to usher in an entirely new approach to art that defined the Renaissance. After Michelangelo, the works of his predecessors and even his contemporaries, save Raphael, became obsolete. Today the Sistine Chapel is inseparable from the name Michelangelo.

Genius always leaves a mark. It separates itself without ever having to speak of its difference. You may not know how to define it, but you know it when you see it. What you see is something you have never seen before. If you are fortunate, it not only changes the way you see the world, it changes you.

In this book, we have looked at the genius of Jesus through the lens of how he engaged with the most profound human dilemmas: the abuse of power, the fight for freedom, the struggle with forgiveness, the path to our most humane selves, and the tension of living up to unattainable human ideals. But the cross was his masterpiece, his Sistine Chapel—a singular event that transcends all time and space and still resonates today.

His decision to save the world through the sacrifice of

his life was nothing short of genius. How do you solve the problem of the human heart if not one person at a time? How do you reconcile all the world to God? Like a fractal that replicates itself over and over again, the death, burial, and resurrection of Jesus replicates itself every time someone turns their heart to him. The cross transports each of us into our own death, burial, and resurrection, showing us against all odds that dying to ourselves can become a way to life. It is the explanation of suffering that our souls long for, and the hope of life beyond the shadow of death.

The cross is the story that words could not tell, the elegant solution to our most complex problems. The cross is tragedy. The cross is beauty. The cross is the genius of Jesus.

It's hard to describe how unlikely this would have been. Before Jesus walked on this planet, the cross was seen in one way and one way only: as a brutal instrument of death. I suppose you could describe it as an expression of Roman genius, if your goal was finding a method of execution that could create the greatest possible suffering, humiliation, and brutality. But for the nations conquered by the Romans, the cross would have been something to fear, not celebrate.

Now, thousands of years later, the cross has become a universal symbol of the sacrifice of God for all humanity. I would argue that it's also the greatest expression of genius humanity has ever known. How can you take the world's greatest instrument of death and forever transform it into the greatest symbol of life?

As with so many other things, Jesus could see what we could not see. When his friends saw him hanging on the cross, all they could see was tragedy. But in one transcendent moment, Jesus not only took a symbol of tragedy and transformed it into a symbol of beauty, he changed the meaning of life and death itself. The time to live and the time to die were no longer separate moments.

No one could have imagined that death would become a way to life. In one moment, Jesus changed our minds about what was possible. He carried all that was good and true and beautiful within himself. He spent his life putting flesh and bone to truth. He became the definition of good. Then he confounded us all by offering himself as a sacrifice for all of us who were far less. In doing so, he made history's most tragic moment eternity's greatest expression of beauty.

I'VE ALWAYS UNDERSTOOD human history as two conflicting narratives weaving themselves together. We have the narrative of beauty and the narrative of tragedy. Solomon describes this in his uniquely poetic way in the book of Ecclesiastes:

There is a time for everything, a season for every ac-
    tivity under the heavens:
a time to be born and a time to die,
a time to plant and a time to uproot,
a time to kill and a time to heal,
a time to tear down and a time to build,
a time to weep and a time to laugh,
a time to mourn and a time to dance,
a time to scatter stones and a time to gather them,
a time to embrace and a time to refrain from em-
    bracing,
a time to search and a time to give up,
a time to keep and a time to throw away,
a time to tear and a time to mend,
a time to be silent and a time to speak,
a time to love and a time to hate,
a time for war and a time for peace.

He goes on to say, "I have seen the burden God has laid on the human race. He has made everything beautiful in its time. He has also set eternity in the human heart, yet no one can fathom what God has done from beginning to end."

This is Solomon's existential crisis. How can one moment be filled with so much pain and another with so much joy? Why is life so often an unbearable contradiction of human emotions and experiences?

In these words, Solomon is reflecting what all of us feel when we face tragedy, or when life is more than we can take. If you have ever wondered, *Why is this happening to me?* you know exactly what I'm talking about. Even when we feel trapped in pain and suffering, there is something transcendent within us that searches to make sense of life against the backdrop of eternity.

In the middle of this crisis of faith, Solomon sees beauty as being singularly important, the thread that weaves all human experience together: "He has made everything beautiful in its time." We know beauty when we experience it: The beauty of your baby's first breath. The beauty of forgiveness undeserved. The beauty of two lovers who have grown old and frail together still walking hand in hand. The beauty of a moment of silence when the world is raging in chaos. But I've learned and seen that the material from which beauty forms its greatest work is often tragedy. It is as if beauty and tragedy are two writers, taking turns to write the novel of our lives.

My friend Makoto Fujimura practices an ancient Japanese art form called kintsugi, in which the artist pours a molten precious metal such as gold into the cracks of a broken piece of pottery. The elegance and beauty emerges as the metal find its way through the cracks. In this way, imperfections become the source of the pottery's uniqueness.

All around us, we can see the beauty of broken things. There is the beauty of the noble death. The beauty of courage when surrounded by violence. The beauty of finding hope when all is lost. The beauty of the struggle to stand when one has fallen. God is the author of beauty, especially when it comes out of chaos. When touched only by the hand of God, all of creation was a paradise. When we took hold of creation, we sent the universe into chaos, and tragedy was introduced into our story.

But the cross forces us to consider, What if beauty isn't supplemental, but essential? What if beauty is not simply a function of adornment, but the material with which we can heal, and extend that healing to others? What if beauty is the end of violence? What if beauty can save the world?

THE ANCIENT GREEKS were one of the earliest recorded cultures to speak of transcendent virtues—the timeless, eternal, intrinsic truths that shape our reality. From Parmenides to Plato, Aristotle to Alexander, their search still shapes our ethics to this day. They identified four cardinal virtues: wisdom, courage, temperance, and justice. They also spoke of "the good, the beautiful, and the true" as being the three transcendentals that inform and elevate all human endeavors. Wherever we find the good and the true, they believed, we would also find beauty.

If Jesus was God, as he claimed he was, then we would

expect him to be the fullness of all that is good and true and beautiful. Yet it was foretold that we would see no beauty in him. Hundreds of years before his birth, here's how Isaiah said the Messiah would be seen by those who awaited him:

He grew up before him like a tender shoot, he had no beauty or majesty to attract us to him, nothing in his appearance that we should desire him.

He was despised and rejected by mankind, a man of suffering, and familiar with pain.

Like one from whom people hide their faces he was despised, and we held him in low esteem.

Did you hear that? There was nothing about Jesus that we would consider attractive, or appealing, or beautiful. How could this be possible? If Jesus was the perfect expression of beauty, how is it possible that we would see no beauty in him at all?

The scriptures seem to be aware of this irony. King David, in one of his psalms, described the experience of looking at God much like we would expect someone to describe seeing the *Mona Lisa* for the first time: "One thing I have asked for the Lord, this only do I seek: that I may dwell in the House of the Lord all the days of my life, to gaze on the beauty of the Lord and to seek him in his temple." David instinctively understood that to look upon God was to be blinded by absolute beauty. Yet these words are in direct contrast to how the people of Israel saw Jesus when he walked among them.

His detractors witnessed God in the flesh, but what they saw was a heretic and a madman. They accused him of being demon-possessed or at best driven by madness. Even those from Jesus's hometown rejected his claims and saw nothing unique or noteworthy about him. They were offended that Jesus would try to distinguish himself. To them, he was nothing more than the son of a carpenter.

This makes me wonder, Is it possible to lose sight of what is beautiful? Is it possible to get so lost in our own tragic story that we give up the possibility that our situation could ever change? If absolute beauty walked right up to us, would we recognize it for what it was, or despise it for what it said about us?

When John, who later became an apostle, first saw Jesus, was he at all impressed? After all, Jesus walked on the scene without pomp, or splendor, or wealth, or fame. There would have been nothing to distinguish him at first sight. He would have been one among so many who worked with their hands and were not afraid of sweat. He was marked by calluses and sun-hardened skin. He was not the product of entitlement or privilege, but of struggle and self-reliance. He would have been muscular from the demands of his work, without any sign of vanity. It was only when he began to speak that he distinguished himself. In spite of his divinity, Jesus was a commoner carrying an uncommon message. The Jesus John saw on the first day they met is not the Jesus he describes to us later when he pens his gospel.

Later, John wrote these words about Jesus: "The Word became flesh and made his dwelling among us. We have seen his glory, the glory of the one and only Son, who came from the Father, full of grace and truth." In this passage, John describes what he and the other disciples saw with their own eyes. But did they really see Jesus's glory from the beginning, or were they blind to it when he first walked among them? Was John only able to write these words after he had seen Jesus risen from the grave? Or did this change of perspective happen three days earlier, when John stood at Jesus's feet as he hung upon a cross?

At the crucible of the cross, John stood at the intersection of beauty and tragedy. On a hill known as Golgotha, he watched as an innocent man asked not for mercy for himself, but for forgiveness and grace for his adversaries and enemies. It was here that John saw the strength of unwavering truth in the midst of lies and false accusations. It was here, and only here, against the backdrop of humanity's darkest moment, that John could see the wonder of the light of the world.

We must not miss the meaning of John's words simply because the language is foreign to us. When the Bible talks about the glory of God, it is describing God's absolute power and beauty. And there is beauty all around us if we have the eyes to see it. There is beauty in the laughter of children, there is beauty in a meal cooked with love, there is beauty in words of kindness gently spoken, there is beauty in the smallest act of compassion. Everything God creates reflects his beauty. The beauty all around you glorifies its Creator. When you see beauty, you are looking at God.

I think we understand this on an intuitive level. All around us in nature, there are endless colors and textures, shapes and sizes, sounds and aromas—an abundance of beauty that overwhelms our senses. We should expect nothing less from the God who is the source and measure of it all. Every artist creates out of their own essence. It is no different for God. Everything God creates is an expression of the unadulterated beautiful. It is simply who he is.

We, too, were created good and true and beautiful. Yet we are now more like a priceless vase that has been dropped and shattered into a million pieces. Our brokenness can be seen in our pain, our fears, our doubts, our desperation, our struggle with loneliness, our sense of insignificance. We know something is missing, something is broken, something is wrong. Only the creator of that vase could understand its intrinsic value. Only its creator would have any hope of restoring it to its original beauty.

There is genius in taking a broken vase and turning it into a mosaic. In seeing a shattered work of art and choosing to accentuate, rather than conceal, its brokenness. To use a material once thought worthless and make it priceless—now that's beautiful.

The answer to our existential questions is transcendence. All the beauty and wonder and mystery of eternity is with you in this moment right now. You are never trapped in a moment. Every moment is a passageway into your future, if you will take it. We do not have all the time in the world, but within time, there is the eternal. And if the God of eternity dwells within you, time is always on your side. The best way to not be overwhelmed by any tragedy is to know that even our pain, and loss, and suffering will become a source of beauty in the end.

WHILE I WAS finishing the manuscript for this book, my family and I escaped for a few days to Mexico. I would write in the mornings and play paddle tennis in the afternoons. It was heaven on earth. We must have played forty hours of heated competition without incident. If I remember correctly, I won more than I lost.

On the last day before we returned to Los Angeles, we had one final match. My son and daughter were my opponents, determined to send me home a loser. The last thing I remember was running to my right and diving for a ball. I remember losing my balance as I began to fall forward. My paddle hit the ground, ricocheted off the court, and hit me directly in the face just under my eye. I laid there for a moment or two, trying to gather myself. I felt sweat pouring down my face that I would later realize was blood gushing from a deep cut.

After seeing several paramedics, two doctors, and one surgeon, I found myself getting fifteen stitches across my face. Even as I write these words, the stitches are still intact and gauze is still covering the wound. I have no idea how pronounced the scar across my face will be when all is said and done.

My sweet wife, Kim, trying to console me, said I could always get plastic surgery to repair my face and conceal my scar. I knew she was just trying to help, but I told her I would keep my scar. I already have quite an array of scars: A surgical scar straight down my abdomen where at the age of twelve my appendix ruptured and almost poisoned me to death. Six scars across my stomach where a robot named da Vinci invaded my body to remove my cancer. A scar across my right arm where a rusted nail awaited me at the end of the long jump pit when I was running track. Scars on my wrists that look like track marks, from my endless trips to doctor's offices and to the hospital as a child. Scars from knee surgery. I could go on and on—and these are just the scars you can see. There are so many that are invisible to the human eye. Scars that mark my soul; that I will bear as long as I walk this earth. The wounds are healed, mind you, but the scars remain.

For the rest of my life, the new scar on my face will greet everyone I meet. But keeping it is the only option. First of all, I've never been that pretty anyway, and I don't trust a man without scars. But most of all, it's a marker of my history. It is a marker of my story. My victories and my defeats. My joy and my pain. My courage and my clumsiness. I will have a scar on my face and it will remind me of who I am. It will help me recognize myself when I look in the mirror. I will wear it with honor. We are known by our scars.

Even Jesus is known by his scars. Especially Jesus.

We are told that three days after Jesus was crucified, on the evening of the first day of the week—which would make it a Sunday—the disciples gathered together. They were still fearful that the same Jewish leaders who had killed Jesus would soon come after them. Their caution led them to meet in a room behind locked doors. It was then that Jesus entered the room and spoke the words that would never be forgotten: "Peace be with you." John goes on to tell us that Jesus showed the disciples the wounds in his hands and his side to confirm that it was him.

We are told that Thomas was not there on that particular evening, and when the other disciples recounted their encounter with Jesus, he was unmoved and refused to believe. He said, "Unless I see the nail marks in his hands, he puts my finger where the nails were, I put my hand into his side, I will not believe."

A week later, the disciples gathered again. Same place, same time, same result. Even though the doors were locked, Jesus once again came among them and greeted them with his declaration, "Peace be with you." Then he turned and looked at Thomas. "Put your finger here," he said. "See my hands? Reach out your hand and put it into my side. Stop doubting and believe." It was then—only then—that Thomas cried out, "My Lord and my God."

Thomas, it seems, could only see the beauty through the scars. Which raises an interesting question: How do you improve on perfection? Scars. Scars that remain in eternity. Why else would Jesus choose to bear his wounds instead of taking care of that during his resurrection? If you can conquer death, surely you could manage a little plastic surgery. Maybe his scars are eternal because they were made by love, and love is eternal. Like Thomas, we will recognize Jesus by his scars. I am grateful he kept them. They're a reminder that he did not simply bring beauty out of our tragedy; he brought beauty into our tragedy. Tragedy no longer has to define us, destroy us, or consume us.

My wife, Kim, has a sister named Renée. They are particularly close, as they were orphaned as children. When Kim was seven years old, she and Renée were placed in a foster home outside Asheville, North Carolina. Renée was two years older than Kim, and all they had in the world was each other. It was a safe home, but a harsh life. They were brought in to help work the family farm, treated more like free labor than labors of love.

Kim toughed it out. She made that home her home and her foster parents her family. Renée eventually ran away and fought to make her own way in the world. In the years to come, Renée became a teenage mom and found herself living in a government housing project. Forty years later, after years of struggling to create a better life, Renée is now the highly respected manager of multiple government housing projects.

Today, she shared with Kim a story that connected our lives from LA to Asheville. On a shift at one of the housing projects, a maintenance worker named Bobby discovered a homeless man living under the porch of one of the apartments. Evidently the man had fallen out with his roommate and could not afford to rent another apartment on his own. He was trying to escape the cold and rain of the mountain in December. Renée had the janitor take him blankets and food so he'd be able to get through the night, but knew she would have to remove him the next morning.

But instead of washing her hands of this man, she spent the evening finding him a place to live. She knew a couple who had recently moved to the Asheville area from California, where they had belonged to Mosaic here in Hollywood. They couldn't believe that Renée was Kim's sister and that they had happened to meet Renée across the country. It's such a small world. She shared the man's story with them and asked if they could help in any way. They offered to take care of the man and pay for him to move into a new apartment. Even as Kim shared this story, I found myself amazed that Renée, the little girl who was homeless and abandoned and surviving in a government project, had become the catcher in the rye in the very place she had needed someone to save her. Her scars became her marks of beauty.

I've seen this narrative play out in the lives of countless people. I've seen it in a defense lawyer who overcame poverty and worked to send himself through law school after his father was wrongly accused of a crime and imprisoned. I've seen it in the child who was traumatized growing up in a high-crime district, where he witnessed the shooting of his brother in a random drive-by. Instead of following a criminal path, he joined the police force to bring safety and peace to his childhood community. Against all odds and expectations, our scars can become our source of beauty.

What if, like Jesus, we were able to see beauty in the tragedy? What if we could create beauty even while we are experiencing tragedy?

What if, suddenly, we saw the world through the eyes of God and knew that all things would be made beautiful in their time?

What if we believed that our very lives were a divine work of art, and we, too, were the beautiful?

Only Jesus could make death beautiful. Only Jesus could bring beauty out of the worst humanity can offer. If nothing else marked the life of Jesus, this one thing would make him the greatest mind who ever lived. He appeared to us as if there was no beauty in him at all, and then made all things beautiful. In the end, this was his greatest work of genius, and his most compelling promise of what our lives could become as well.

SEVERAL YEARS AGO, I spoke to a journalist from New York. She was doing a story on spirituality among millennials and why they were becoming open to faith. At one point in the interview, she paused and asked a question that seemed less for the article and more for herself. She had already described herself to me as a person without faith, and I could tell she was struggling for the right language. "What does it feel like to believe in God?" she finally asked.

I liked this journalist. I liked her a lot. I sensed she was sincere and inquisitive and open, and I thought hard before responding. When you've been doing this as long as I have, you begin to feel the longing inside a person. It felt like someone who is blind asking you to help them understand color, or someone who is deaf desperate to experience sound. I knew she was taking a risk. Maybe I had actually experienced God. Maybe I could help her know what that feels like. Maybe I could help her recognize it if it ever happened to her.

My answer went something like this: It doesn't feel like anything to believe in God, but let me describe the best I can how it feels to *know* God. Have you ever been so in love that it changes how you see and experience everything? Suddenly all your senses are heightened. Colors are brighter and more beautiful. Aromas explode in your nostrils and flavors overwhelm your taste buds. You become aware of the wonder of everything, and with every breath, you are fully alive.

It can be overwhelming. You will be overwhelmed by all the beauty all around you. It might feel as if it's more than you can bear. This is what it's like to know God. It's breathtakingly beautiful. It leaves you breathless; it makes you wonder how it's possible that you once were completely unaware of it. It weighs on you how tragic it is that all the world cannot see such beauty. All they see is the heartbreak and devastation of a world seemingly in ruins. All the while, you think to yourself that it doesn't take a genius to see all this beauty. Or maybe it does.

Acknowledgments

My journey of studying genius and searching for God has stretched the length of my life. *The Genius of Jesus* is my attempt to put into words the extraordinary impact the person of Jesus has made on my life, and on the history of humanity. I could not have written this book without the incredible people who show me what genius looks like in a thousand different ways.

I want to thank Esther Fedorkevich and the Fedd Agency for believing in me and the message of *The Genius of Jesus*.

To Tina Constable and my team at Convergent, your support has allowed this book to find life in physical form.

Derek Reed, thank you for your input and direction throughout the editing process.

I want to thank my leadership and creative teams at Mosaic. Together we have won many victories and weathered many storms. Thank you for your support and your tireless efforts to share the mission and man of Jesus with the world. I see genius in the way each of you shares his love and grace with our city and with people around the world.

Thank you to Brooke Figueroa, for all of the incredible help you have given me in refining this book. You have been essential to the process.

I also want to thank Alisah Duran, who provides invaluable service to our team here in LA in more ways than I can measure.

To my mom, your exploration of faith paved the way for me to find the faith I desperately longed for. Thank you for always being willing to step first into the unknown.

To my wife, Kim, and our kids, Aaron, Mariah and Jake, and Paty and Steve: You have been living proof to me of the genius God has placed inside every person. It has been a great privilege to witness each of your genius find its way to the forefront of your lives.

Most of all, I must thank the one who showed humanity what it meant to be human again. Thank you, Jesus, for offering your life in sacrifice so that I would find life. Thank you for living a life of pure genius and then sharing that genius with all who would carry the mantle of your name.

Acknowledgments

You gave me hope that my life could have purpose and meaning, because you are the source of purpose and the author of meaning. You are truly the greatest genius the world will ever know, and yet you make yourself fully known to all who seek you. I love you.

ABOUT THE AUTHOR

ERWIN RAPHAEL MCMANUS has committed his life to the study of genius and the pursuit of God, never knowing that the two worlds would one day collide. He is an iconoclast, entrepreneur, storyteller, fashion designer, filmmaker, and cultural thought leader whose singular intention is to violate our view of reality. McManus is the founder of Mosaic, a church movement based in the heart of Hollywood with a community that spans the globe, and is the acclaimed author of *The Way of the Warrior, The Last Arrow,* and other leading books on spirituality and creativity. His books have sold more than a million copies worldwide, in fourteen different languages. McManus studied philosophy at Elon University and has a bachelor of arts in psychology from the University of North Carolina at Chapel Hill, a master of divinity from Southwestern Theological Seminary, and a doctorate of humane letters from Southeastern University. He lives in Los Angeles, California, with his wife, Kim McManus.

erwinmcmanus.com

ORIGINS BY MOSAIC

DIVE   DEEPER   INTO
THE   GENIUS   OF   JESUS

/

AND MORE CONTENT FROM
ERWIN RAPHAEL MCMANUS

ERWINMCMANUS.COM/ORIGINS